Sound, Movement and Tears

Cynthia Herman

Earth Mirth Adventure
Peoria, Illinois

Precious Earthen Sister —
Wheat a joy to recommend book
home with Big Red Meema —
Stay in touch
Love,
Cindy Houch

Disclaimer

This collection of inspired words is not meant to be a guide to choosing therapy, diet, physical assistance or medical guidance of any type. None of the narrative contained herein should be substituted for professional services – legal, medical or other. This book, Sound, Movement and Tears, is offered to convey one woman's understanding and her experiences of healing. As such, it is not meant to portray the only methods to glorious health; you must choose your own. If any expert assistance is required, the services of a competent professional should be sought. This is an extremely personal matter and each individual must choose his or her own way. A conversation with a trusted and competent professional is advised, but the ultimate decisions must be yours alone. If you do not wish to be bound by this disclaimer, you may return this book to the publisher for a full refund.

Godspeed...

Requests for permission should be addressed to:

Earth Mirth Adventure
P.O. Box 4231
Peoria, IL 61607
www.earthmirth.com

Published in the United States by:

Altarfire Publishing
1835 Oak Terrace
Newcastle, California

Publisher's Cataloging-in-Publication:
(Provided by *Quality Books, Inc.*)
Herman, Cynthia.
    Sound, movement and tears/ by Cynthia Herman
 -- 1st ed.
    p. cm
    LLCN: 99-90772
    ISBN: 0-9655558-0-1

    1. New Thought. 2. Mental healing.
    3. Self-help techniques. 4. Health--Religious
    aspects--New Age Movement. 5. Metaphysics.
    I. Title.

BF639.H47 1999   299'.93
                                QB199-1207

Cover Design by Roger Strand
Cover Photo by Mel Waters
Dedication Photo by Gregory Holland
Printed in the United States of America

ACKNOWLEDGEMENTS

I want to thank God who, through me, wrote this book. I put off writing a post card for months because I dread so the act of writing, but this book was, basically, done in 3 weeks. In the following years, I awoke with ideas; each addition tripled my esteem for authors and matured my innocent gratitude for those three blissful weeks in the blizzard.

Sincere and ancient gratitude to P'taah who reminded me again of what I know.

I also want to thank three remarkable men, Frank Strand, Roger Strand and Harry Simmon. If it hadn't been for their Olympian generosity, this book could not have been written.

A hugful of thank-yous to Kent and Margie Williams, editors extraordinaire. They know well about inspired writing. As Picasso said, "A great painter knows when to quit." Their egolessness allowed them to keep the manuscript intact, with the suggestions and composition of an artist.

The Alaskan Iditarod would have been luxury to me compared to transfering this into a computer but after countless excruciating and hilarious hours, being dragged kicking and screaming through computerdom, two pillars of patience, Joe Fitzanko and Mary LoPicallo, masterfully electrified the text. I'm in awe.

To my Earth Mother
and my earthen mother, Angeline,
who was the fertile soil
for unconditional love
by masquerading as
my greatest challenge.

Her leaving my side
is the river of tears
that will one day wash me clean
and fulfill the promise
I've made her.

CONTENTS
Sound, Movement and Tears
Cynthia Herman

AUTHOR'S INTRODUCTION

After the Julliard School and a successful career of performing with dozens of fine actors, I made a discovery that I thought was fascinating, and began twenty years of observing. For three weeks in January of 1998, this book poured effortlessly forth, and I take little credit for writing it.

This was my discovery: The body's natural reaction to pain is sound, movement and tears. How often as adults do we do this?

The mistake we've made for hundreds of years is assuming that emotions are mental. They're not — they're a physical change in our cells. All the intellect, will-power and morality we can muster will not make them go away.

A healthy body has balanced cells, and their vibration causes a sound. When an emotion washes over us, the vibration of our cells shifts, causing a new sound to be made. The gut instinct response to pain is to cry or utter a moan. (We feel very free to make sound and movement if the emotion is one of excitement.) If we don't restore the balance of the cell through sound, movement or tears, it will remain at a slower rate of vibration, contributing to overweight and all our diseases.

We have the potential for 64 DNA and only 20 are "turned on." Do you know, basically, what turns on DNA? E-motion. Energy in motion. When energy is stopped it creates pressure. If we don't ex press the pressure out, we will re-press, op-press, and de-press. There's a lot we don't know about this cryptic power, but perhaps we should begin the research.

Emotion is our driving force, our power source, our motor. Used consciously, we can create a heaven on earth; used unconsciously, we dwell in hell. Isn't it time to get conscious?

This material came through in meter, a rhythm to every sentence. I apologize if the style seems foreign; it might help to approach it as a poem. Whether or not we're aware of it, rhythm gracefully brings us home, because it's the language of the heart and the earth and the uni-*verse* from which we come.

I speak often and fondly of Jesus, because he was a master metaphysician and I've been in love with him since Sunday School. But the Laws in this book far transcend any religion, psychology or biology.

Twenty years ago in the Taos Pueblo, I bought some wood shaped like an ear and my prayer was that I might Hear. If these words are helpful to anyone, I'll know my prayer has been answered.

Hearts of fire,

Cynthia Herman
September 9, 1999

Chapter 1

TV to Teepee

Let me give you a little background into what my life has been like, so you can better understand why I write this. I was born 50 years ago in Peoria, Illinois. From the moment I imitated the Fig Newton commercial and heard the family laugh, I knew I wanted to act.

After college I was accepted into the newly formed drama division of the Julliard School in New York. The man in charge was John Houseman (you know him from the TV commercial "the old-fashioned way, we 'earrrrn' it") and as students he demanded that we "earrrrn" any merit bestowed. It was very exciting and challenging because all of us, the students, the teachers, even John himself, were creating something brand new – a school and a nationally touring acting company.

It was hilarious fun to tour the U.S. with my close and crazy friends: Kevin Kline, Patti LuPone, David Ogden Stiers and others of as great a talent who've chosen a quieter fame. Each member of the company was and is a star and I love them more than words can say.

After that I did *Anyone for Tennyson?*, reading poetry on PBS, and over 50 national television commercials (my "Fig Newton" persona paid off). I moved to L.A. and continued my career with plays, commercials and pilots. I worked with Meryl

Streep, Glenn Close, Jack Lemmon, Henry Fonda and dozens of very fine actors. But the strain of living in New York and L.A. ultimately took its toll and I knew I needed bare feet on the ground to feel my Midwestern roots.

Returning to Illinois again, I bought an old farmhouse on eight acres of land with no plumbing, no TV and no stress. I planted a garden, harvested and canned, chasing chickens, a goose and a goat. It was heaven. After three lovely years when the money ran out, I realized I had to scale down. So I built from scratch a 12-foot teepee and set it up in the Blue Ridge Mountains. That was too.

Daily on the farm, and in the silence of the mountains, I felt tension drain from my limbs. I found myself crying inconsolably over past criticisms from school and critics, the thoughtless appraisals of directors and auditioners and the natural rejection of the business... sorrow I had no idea was there.

But I noticed I was changing. My voice had lowered, my shoulders realigned and my stomach and back pain decreased.

Then one night at a party in Peoria, a discovery made it all quite clear. As an actor, one studies emotion – not just visually, but empathetically – experiencing what humanity feels. I saw that God had removed me from acting to observe from a new perspective... no longer from how to imitate, but from – possibly – how to heal.

Chapter 2

From The Mouths of Babes
"Natural forces within us
are the true healers of disease." [1]

I was having a fine time at my sister's dinner party when I went to use the ladies room off a bedroom. (Ladies, if you didn't know, are carriers of water – especially if it's their favorite drink, occasionally mixed with Guinness Stout.) I knew that our friend had put her baby in there, so I didn't turn on the light. I didn't realize, in the absence of a crib, she'd lain him on the floor, and in the dark, to my horror, I hit the infant with my foot. Before I continue, gentlepeople, the baby turned out fine. But for his experiencing two minutes of pain, I shall always feel hugely indebted.

I immediately held him in my arms for comfort and this is what I observed: His back arched as far as possible and he screamed at the top of his lungs. (Luckily this was a big house and we were quite a distance from the rest.) At the end of his breath, he arched again and screamed with his fullest force, tears flowing down his cheeks. Again he arched and screamed and wept, each scream a note lower than the previous.

After about one minute of full-scale screaming and crying, each lessening in length and intensity, he settled into a whimper and sniffling that

---

[1] Hippocrates

11

lasted for another minute. Then, to my amazement, he was fast asleep in my arms.

I was dumbfounded by the simplicity of what I had just observed. The body's natural reaction to pain is sound, movement and tears. How often as adults do we do this?

I remembered the law of physics: "Energy never disappears, it simply changes its form." The force of that blow in the baby's side changed into sound, movement and tears and the infant was clearly at peace. I thought back over my own deep weeps – how similar to that baby's they'd been. I hadn't been kicked, but the identical reaction had occurred from emotional blows.

And I got to thinking: If I'm not transforming an emotional blow into sound, movement and tears, what is that energy becoming? Illness, anger, stress, hate, unhappiness, overweight?

Chapter 3

To Thine Own Self Be True

If your parents were Mary and Joseph, then this book is not for you. Every parent honestly wants to do the best they can, but often with the best intentions, they unknowingly cause harm and because of that, we hurt.

But how the hurt got there doesn't interest me too much. It can lead to destructive blame. No, I prefer to liken it to discovering a lion in your house. Would you stand there and wonder "Now how did he get in? Was it the front door, the back door or the window? Was it while we were eating or sleeping? Did Margie or Sandra or Pam let him in?" WHO CARES! GET THE LION OUT OF THE HOUSE! No, this book is not about blame, it's about acknowledging the pain.

God chose, when He designed this plan, to speak to us through our emotions because He knew the rational brain would not develop for thousands of years. Our first reaction to an event before us occurs in the amygdala brain, which stimulates our instincts and impulses, telling us what's good and what's bad. This pure energy of *experience*, like a horse prodded left or right, or for us "move forward or away", was our primary mode of guidance. Yet today we relegate our instinctive knowing, "emotional consciousness", to the role of repressed subconscious. This book suggests we reverse pattern if we want to achieve a healing.

The word *holy* comes originally from *whole*. How can we be whole or holy if we deny half of our instincts? We've bought into the belief that God only loves us when we are positive and nice and dislikes us when we're negative because that's how we were treated by our parents. But how ridiculous! *He* was the one who gave us those feelings to guide us wisely through life.

Jesus exhibited all the emotions. He was so angry in the temple at the moneylenders that He knocked their tables over. He was so terrified at the thought of dying that He begged God to 'pass the cup'. He was so sad over leaving this world that He walked off alone and wept. If we are made in the image of God, then God must have these feelings. In fact, emotion is the state in which we are closest to the Divine— it is pure unadulterated **energy** – our *Soul*. Thought is secondary and inferior – it is slowed-down, densified feeling. We all want to have an experience of God, yet we spend most of our time thinking. If emotions are our soul and we acknowledge only half of them (the *nice* ones), no wonder we're disconnected to God. When we understand that our lives are guided by emotions we're not even aware of, isn't that reason enough to get conscious?

If we didn't have negative feelings, we'd die – an abuser could continue his abuse. They're a shiver divine declaring which actions will benefit and which ones will not. A positive feeling leads to life enhancement – and a negative to life destruction. *(Evil* is *live* spelled backward.) Now this is where the rational comes in – tempering these instincts with reason. "If I eat six chocolate sundaes, my life will not be enhanced." Or, "If I sleep with Charlene, my best friend's girl, my wife will not be enhanced."

We feel with our instincts, then reason out the results. But we make the mistake of assuming that negative feelings have no message. "Anger is my enemy and it always gets me in trouble, so I'll pretend like it didn't happen." But emotion is the will, the power... the energy to get things done, to either continue the positive actions or change the ones that aren't.

When you're standing in the grocery store and you hear a woman slap her child, that anger that just rippled through you is God saying, "Do something to improve this." You go over and calmly say to the mom, "I have a good idea. Maybe he could have the candy if he helps you with the dishes", or some other suggestion to solve the problem in a pleasant and non-threatening way. Maybe this anger provided a chance to change two people's lives.

If the slap really made you furious, I suggest you go out to your car and shout into your hand all the fierceness you wanted to say to her. (If you stay with anger long enough, it will hopefully turn into tears. Behind 90% of the anger we feel is a hurting, sorrowful child. Most rage, aggression and "acting out" are a mask for forbidden tears. That's why the studies of people punching a bag in an effort to discharge anger provided inconclusive results. Sound and tears, the elements most transformative, in my experience of twenty years, were excluded.)

If you then can be calm, approach her, if not, just walk away, thanking her for the chance to heal. Because she made you **feel** something and **whenever we feel we heal.**

Realize this: **Negative events happen as opportunities to release emotion.**

Why does a person say after 15 years since divorce that she still can't get it off her mind? Our impatient suggestions brutally include: Snap out of it! Get over it! Move on! But the child in her is wiser than that – it knows what she must do first. She must shed all the tears of the pain of that loss to restore her body to balance. That's why it haunts her – she has unfinished business – what's missing is not her husband; it's the tears and shouting, deeply buried, that must find their way to the light. If she has the courage to walk that dark road, a radiant new life will unfold.

Because, you see, we all have rage – the rage that Jesus had. When someone says sanctimoniously to me, "Oh, I have no anger toward them." after relating a hair-raising horror story they've just been thrashing through, my heart wants to break and weep for them because I hear deep denial, and it ain't the river in Egypt. I suspect what that denial might cost them – breast cancer, heart attacks, disease.

Emotion is not a mental choice. It's a physical change in our cells (chapter 9).

Our mind can successfully repress it but we're foolish if we think we've erased it. Saying "Don't be angry" is as silly as saying: "Don't be white." "Don't be black." "Don't be female." The physical reality exists.

It is so inculcated in our formative years that we are bad when we are angry or sad and from the pain of our parents withdrawing their love, we quickly learn to adapt. We learn to repress those ugly monsters that will only get us in trouble. And by the time we are forty or fifty, we've gotten so skilled at avoiding the taboos, ignoring the many, mini-dramas that go on, daily, in our unconscious mind, that we quite sincerely and truthfully mean it when we say, "I feel no anger."

But I can almost promise you, if you are stressed or isolated, overweight or sick, you are withholding negative energy.

Jesus was a human and He expressed each of these feelings. And hello, you're human too.

And if you've been thinking it's better not to feel, then draw your own conclusions: You must be better than Jesus. (Or are you, possibly, just less truthfu?)

Chapter 4

Cry Is Most of Christ's Name

I have been crying for twenty years now, sometimes waking in the night to weep, and why, I am not sure. Recently I came upon a Rilke poem, "and one day if we are patient, we will live into the answers" which reminded me, I needn't try to know why. I do know that I love my life and I love all of God's creation. And with that gift comes the silent vow to somehow, some way, serve. And since we're all connected by sheer, translucent lines, perhaps I am crying for someone who is hurting and doesn't know how to let go.

Scientists have told us tears contain toxins, which if not released, cause disease. To cry is to purify. And don't you feel better after a good, hearty cry? That weight you've been carrying disappears. Some people tell me they feel worse afterwards. I suspect that's because unconsciously they feel guilty, that they shouldn't be such a 'wimp', so the brakes are on through the process. The mixed messages – "I shouldn't be crying, but I'm going to anyway" – cause a painful headache and can be avoided by knowing its healing effect. By shifting our perspective from denial to acceptance, these waters can wash us clean.

In some tribal regions of Africa, when a woman's husband dies, the neighboring villages gather around to assist her with all the chores. For two weeks the widow purges all of her sorrow with sobbing and wailing and moaning, her anger, frustration and guilt – there is no feeling that is incorrect that arises with a loved one's loss. Is grief over then after two weeks, or six – six months or a year? Are we foolish to name a time?

For some, it will be soon – for others, long, depending on the depth of the loss. And that's okay. Going on with life shouldn't mean denial, but rather accepting the loss and the pain as expressions of how much you loved them; not closing down, but opening our hearts and embracing the grief as it leaves.

When Mother Theresa and Diana died, a major shift on the planet occurred. They were using their influence to better the world, and their warm and affectionate manner of communicating was starkly contrasted to 'royalty'. They represented sensitivity and compassion: qualities we demand now from our leaders. Never before in the history of the world has there been such a collective mourning. It was estimated a billion people gathered to watch the funerals.

When many minds focus on a single event it exponentially increases it for us all. Together we felt and wept and mourned, them and our own deep losses. It lifted a heavy veil from our hearts, and from the heart of Mother Earth, because we are intimately connected. Their lives were dedicated to service — who suspected that their deaths would be such Gift?

And that's true of our loved ones as well – their life has been a great blessing to us – can we accept the favor death brings? Part of their leaving was sacrifice, to offer you the benefaction of mourning. *If the pain of their loss doesn't knock you to your knees then the gift of their going is gone.* The tears it should cause can transform us with the profoundest humility and surrender.

The highest tribute you can give a departed is to ask God to help you express all that sorrow that will elevate both you and your beloved. Because you are still intimately connected; the work you do on your own evolution positively affects the departed.

Is it surprising then, that *mourning* is also the word *morning*?

I was fortunate, like thousands of others, to receive a pendant from Mother Theresa. She sat there for hours handing them out with a radiant smile on her face. Where did that joy, that peace, come from? She hadn't dined at the Ritz with the finest champagne, something we'd like to do to get happy. She'd spent years shedding tears over the maimed and the sick, the hurting, the helpless, the fallen.

And Jesus – think of the tears that were spent as He walked through the world of the poor, the diseased and the dying. We think it's a blessing in America that we rarely encounter deep need, but perhaps it's a curse that our lives are protected, so insulated, hygienic and safe. Except for some pictures of starvation on TV, we don't have many chances to feel humanity's dire need. If we did, it would hurt us, and move us, and change us – the way that it did to Jesus. He couldn't have witnessed a lifetime of sorrow without weeping a river of tears.

"Pain carves the well that will hold all our joy."

I'm not saying that it's holier in Calcutta and Damascus than dining on champagne at the Ritz. I'm saying that something extraordinary happens when we open our hearts to the hurt. Our willingness to release our own hidden pain sensitizes us to the pain of others. Is that maybe why we hesitate? That can of worms, that Pandora's box is better left unopened?

I'm suggesting that the opposite is true. That peace and joy and our heart's full treasure lie at the bottom of that box. And it's only through struggling with the worms and the snakes that we are finally able to claim it.

A SUMMARY OF THE WORLD (1997)

If we could, at this time, shrink the Earth's population to a village of 100 people, with all existing human ratios remaining the same, it would look something like this:

- There would be 57 Asians, 21 Europeans, 14 from the Western Hemisphere (North and South) and 8 Africans.

- 70 of the 100 would be non-white.

- 70 of the 100 would be non-Christian, 30 Christian.

- 50% of the entire world's wealth would be in the hands of only 6 people. All 6 would be citizens of the United States.

- 70 of the 100 would be unable to read.

- 50 would suffer from malnutrition.

- 80 would live in a substandard housing.

Love has a hem to her garment
that reaches the very dust.
It sweeps the lanes
and by-ways clean,
and because it can,
it must.

Mother Theresa

Chapter 5

Go To Your Room! Redefined

Feelings don't want to ruin our lives, they simply want to be felt. Successful psychologist Gay Hendricks, in his book *Learning to Love Yourself*, writes that after years of talking through problems, he wished he could be more effective, so he went out into nature and asked God for help. He felt an electricity from his feet to his head and was given quite an answer: ***Feelings cannot be talked away, they can only be felt away.***

While sharing that with his patients, he discovered the added benefit of releasing; after expressing a muffled emotion, a solution very often arises. By leaving our logic to instead, feel, we tap into creative intuition. I've experienced this countless times – as soon as I'm willing to feel out the pain, an idea for improvement emerges.

How can we apply his amazing realization to improving the quality of our lives? Let's go back to when we were small. Mistreatment is much more complex than simply being slapped or hit. Civilized people have been taught not to strike and pride themselves on their restraint.

But unfortunately, what they choose to do is far and away more insidious. They retreat and withhold their love. I would define mistreatment as the act of withdrawing our love.

Both methods, withdraw or hit, are experienced by children as abuse. So as parents, we must make it our goal to always stay connected. I know you want that, and perhaps it sounds impossible, but I've experienced a process that works.

When our children try our patience and we want to yell or withdraw, we are basically giving the message *"Beware*, you're pushing my buttons and I want to shout and cry, and *I know* I can't do that, so *back off."*

Well, I'm here to suggest that you can. Not only can, but you'd better and you'd better be doing it quickly. You're doing to your child what your parents did to you because they didn't know how NOT to. No one knew how *Not* to.

Here's how Not to:

Step 1: Never throw your anger at people. Universal Law #1, "Everything we do comes back to us". You don't want to see this on your doorstep, but without question, you will. (Look at the word against – you will be seeing this again.) "Somehow, somewhere, just when you least expect it," rather like Candid Camera.

Step 2: Throw your head out the window. That's right, very important. Do not proceed without Step 2. (The truth is you can't – it's impossible.) Your brain will immediately talk you out of it, intellectualizing the feelings away. "I'll get hit or beaten or worse if I do." "I'm a bad person, so I'll be good." "Mom/Dad/God will hate me." "I don't want to be a cry baby." "I'll be strong and not feel this." are just a few in the arsenal of excuses we use to avoid the beasties.

But, winning the trophy for rationalism will not make it go away. You can talk your way to the moon and back, but a "charge" is not being released. If talking was the only solution to emotional and physical pain, then babies would have to be orators for civilization to survive! They're not, they scream, and they scream real loud because they know *the sound is the healing – to feel is to heal.* Remember physics and energy; it is going to change its form and what, I suspect, it wants to change into is sound, movement and tears. So instead of being a logical, adult, we're going to become a child. The four-year-old that's been waiting within is *finally* going to be heard.

You can do this – it's being an actor. It's feeling an emotion and expressing it. (I think our fascination with actors is because we each know we *are* one, deep down – that there is such a plethora of drama in there that, easily, we could sway the masses.) And wouldn't it feel wonderful to finally get all those bothersome bugaboos out?

Yes, it does! It's a tremendous relief when it's over. It's the high after a performance. Our cells are vibrating at a faster rate due to the discharge of negative energy. (chapter 9.) That's why actors go into acting, I think, to unconsciously perform a healing for ourselves and for the audience. (Also we're not very good at *real* jobs, and the money, too, is good.)

Theater began on the steps of the church and the word could be translated 'seeing God'. Someone must have noticed back then, that when we feel, we heal, and it was difficult for most people to do that. So they found a few weirdos who could easily emote and offered the audience a catharsis. As the actor felt his rage and sorrow, the audience felt theirs out, too. A resonance of emotion occurred that purged and purified.

That's what TV and films do now – they make us laugh and cry and scream – catharsis that keeps us well.

(Sorry for that digression.)

Step 3: Connect to a higher power, however you define that – God, Spirit, Great Spirit, etc. This step is not optional, you *will* need help and help of the highest order. (It amazes me to think that someone would try to do life without it, without the countless joys and healing that it generously, daily offers.)

Step 4: Begin breathing deeply – it allows the feelings to surface. Shallow breathing is a habit we've developed to keep our emotions repressed. This works for some people but not for others – if you find it increases the feeling, continue. If not, go on to step 5.

Step 5: Find a secluded corner where no one will be disturbed, and get a pillow to yell into. Pretend that the negative influence in your life, your mother, your father, your brother, whoever, is seated in a chair before you and open up and let 'er rip –remember you're four. You can say things that are mean and stupid and cruel and unfair and false.

You don't have to make sense, you just have to make feelings. (Here's where cursing and swearing are useful, but only for private use.) You can hit the bed or couch or chair, stab or slap or stomp, (yelling into your hand or pillow makes no noise). The *pressure* of the pain inside is seeking a complete release so imagine ex-press-ing it on others. (If we don't ex-press, we'll re-press, de-press, or sup-press.)

And if tears come, that's the Blessing. (Its *safer* to be angry since we are still in control and it's scary to be vulnerable and open – so tears usually hide behind anger.) Stay with it as long as you want. Get out every sob and threat that wants to finally be freed. And if you discover there's more to escape, commit to it again. Completing the process might take months or years, but each time you do it, you heal.

And then, when your daughter irritates you again, you won't get emotional or withdraw. The sorrow and rage from your own damaged childhood was released on the bed and the pillow. And you won't have the need to expel it on her or separate yourself from her love. When she's having a problem you'll react more objectively – and be able to listen and support her.

27

Now this doesn't mean there's no discipline. Teaching a child to respect his emotions doesn't free him from being accountable. But let's quit saying "Don't be angry, scared, or sad." Feelings are how we evolve and learn, and "Don't" says "Ignore half of them." The only Don't we need to underscore is "Don't ever use your feelings to harm." Screaming and yelling in public places or in mother's face is unacceptable. When they are angry say "I understand. It's okay to be angry, but only in a private place." Teach them how to release the charge in the way you've taught yourself.

When your child is crying, for whatever reason, don't devalue it if it isn't logical. If you do he'll think that emotions are allowed *only* if they make good sense.

But ***logic won't erase our pain – feeling it out will.*** Just comfort him and encourage the tears saying "I know – that makes me sad too." (You're teaching him empathy – that it's important to feel what other's feel.) "It's okay to be sad and cry." Then hold him closely till the tears are spent and he'll be much more open to your wisdom.

When your child is frightened, be near to console him and say "I know, I understand – I'd be scared too. It's okay to be scared, it's natural. But you know what? God has given you a guardian angel who will always watch over you and protect you, and mommy and daddy will, too."

These are simplifications, of course, that you will tailor to your individual needs. But we must teach our children to respect *all* feelings and express them in appropriate ways.

Can we visualize the potency of this? If harming our children comes from when *we* were harmed, can we imagine the peace in this world, if each of us were willing to embrace our inner child and finally begin honoring its feelings? And teach our children that every emotion is from God and deserves our respect?

To admit is to open a door. To not admit is to keep it closed. How many generations will need to repeat the ancient and painful pattern before we admit our own hidden darkness and open the door to the light?

Chapter 6

Stressed Is Desserts Backwards

Here's how I define stress: The effort required to re-Press emotion. *STRESS = REPRESS.* 'Emote' means to move toward, yet we desperately move away. We exhaust ourselves in an effort to escape a forbidden negative feeling. On a very unconscious level we're thinking, "I'm so mad I could scream my head off, but I'm *not* going to feel it." Liken it to pushing on a dam all day to hold back an oncoming river.

Men used to lead the field in heart attacks because of the stress in the workplace. Now women who have entered into business careers are joining them in this disease. The office obviously creates more pressures with less chance to relax than the home.

The usual prescriptions for stress are these: Breathe deeply, count to ten, soak in the tub, relax with music, do yoga or meditation. And all of these are wonderful, but they ultimately won't solve the problem.

Unless you react to the stress in your life like that infant I held long ago, *something* is not being released. That baby wasn't capricious – he had a clear and determined intent and the result of his action brought peace.

Now you could say, "That baby was hit, I just got an emotional blow". Well, I would say, look at a four-year-old when you tell him you're not going to the zoo, after promising it for a week. Did you hit him? No. What's he doing? He's kicking and crying and screaming. Like the Puritans, will we condemn him for his "evil, wayward soul"? Or will we find in his spontaneity a clue to what's missing in us?

Let's imagine now that you're at work and Sally the Shark walks by and zings you with yet another of her cunningly crafted insults. Unbeknownst to you, your stomach starts burning. (That's why Zantac is so popular.) But your well-trained brain kicks into gear and immediately talks you out of it. "Who, Sally? She's an idiot, why would I bother about her?"

In fact, possibly one of our favorite prides as the 'civilized' folks of the Earth, is how we nobly rise above our 'foul and unclean passions'. We encapsulate and bury them in our 'goodly, godly and polite' closet and smile beatifically after another hard won victory over the 'fiery influence of the devil!'

Well, I will agree it wouldn't have been good to slap Sally's sneering face off. But how infinitely more evil to lie to yourself – and to Sally and to God – and pretend like it didn't hurt. That fire that you felt was from none other than God, charging you to change some behavior. Respect the spark and acknowledge the message by letting it burn on through as a flash of wisdom toward greater enlightenment, "I won't let this happen again."

So you'll talk to Sally some time today, in a calm and effective manner, telling her how you feel, not how you think – she can't refute your emotions. Stay with the feeling, don't attack her behavior; just honestly tell her how you feel. But, before you do, you'll have gone to your car and proceeded to slap her silly. You'll yell into your hand every insult and threat you've wanted to say since you met her. You'll have released the emotion that was causing the stress of *working to not let it out*.

We take a shower every day to clean our physical body. Couldn't we take an emotional bath to daily clean that dirt? I call it *SMuT* (sound, movement and tears). Life is not perfect, people are not always kind. Their less-than-lovely comments harm us whether we know it or not. The daily put-downs, the unkind jokes, the coldness, the separation, the innuendoes and, most insidious, cynicism. It masquerades as intellect, superior and cool, but each dig, a mini-death for hope and optimism and grace.

Suggestion: Find a picture of yourself when you were small. See how open, vulnerable, and trusting you were? The greatest reward of a daily cleanse is the ability to return to that state. Enclose it in plastic and keep it in your pocket or your purse, or on the fridge or your desk. Realize that child still lives within, not reasoning, not thinking, *just feeling*. He has the key to your survival because he knows how to get stress-free. It doesn't matter if you are 20 or 80, be willing to act like you're 3.

Commit some time to a cleanse each day –
you'll be amazed at the rapidity of your progress.
There's nothing I know of that's free and harmless, yet so effective in healing all ills. Keeping a
journal of your daily releasing is also powerful; it
brings the unconscious to the conscious. Record,
each day, what happens, what was said, what was
done, what was felt.

You'll be amazed looking back – after just
one month – how surprisingly far you've come.
Name it perhaps "The African Queen" or "Travers-
ing the Treacherous Waters of my Cleverly, Closeted Quagmire." (Releasing all this seriousness will
increase your sense of mirth.)

Start noticing how your body feels in the
presence of different people, how positive people
uplift you – and negative ones depress. Avoid those
if you can. If you can't, be aware of how bad they've
made you feel; then, when taking your shower, yell
into your hand and get yourself really clean. Or, if
the day's been dreadfully rough, get a plastic bat
from the dimestore and slaughter the arm of your
chair. (Privately, of course. This is between you,
your boss, and the chair.)

In other words, become body-wise, by listening to the signals it's giving. When you get
alone-time, ask your body the question, "What
did I feel when she said that?" Name it. "I felt
angry." Now, the next thing is very important.
Say "It's *okay* to be angry; I love all the feelings I
feel." Then take out the photo of yourself as a
child and ask "What does this feeling make me
want to *do*? I want to hit him and kick him and
scream, 'I hate your guts'."

Find a private place where you won't disturb and *do* it. (And try to get in touch with the tears – most anger is a facade for sorrow.) Take this process slowly at first – our 'can of worms' can be awesome. Keep enough of your head on your shoulders to protect your emerging child.

Look at the words 'heart attack'. Our heart literally has to attack us to get the attention it deserves. "You've asked me to carry all this pain for years and I'm sick of the weight and the pretense."

Native Americans have a saying: "Call a ghost by its name and it will go away." Now that we know a harmless way to do this, do we have the courage to begin? To illuminate the corners of a burdened heart and name all our fearful demons? After we've freed them, we wisely observe that they weren't as frightening as we'd thought. The only danger was our foolishly thinking that *silent* they would remain.

Chapter 7

"The Sun Shines Not On Us But In Us" [1]

Of all the things that Jesus said, this one fascinates me the most. "What I have done, you will do too – and more of". Staggering, when you think of that. What did He have that we don't have? Well, yes, He was the son of God. But the way I interpret His message is that you and I are too. "Oh, no!" you say, "He was different, perfect." creating that popular separation between church and state, God and man, us and Jesus. But it's that very separation that is causing the misery and suffering in this world.

I think, like Jesus, we could be performing miracles and it's true there are some each day. But why isn't it a common occurrence, like Jesus long ago predicted?

Well, every theologian, I strongly suspect, has a weighty and educated opinion. But, allow me to offer a theory I've considered since I watched that baby cry. The infant was being *truthful* about what it was he was feeling. A child will honestly scream and kick when we take away his toy. All through the Bible is the oft-repeated *truth*, and I don't remember frequently seeing *nice, polite* and *sweet*.

---

[1] John Muir

All over this planet, in the presence of pain, a baby, a toddler, the mentally ill, an animal will react with sound, movement and tears. They have not learned how to lie. I believe our diseases, our neuroses and our misfortunes are based upon that lie.

"Give up your burdens to me." What greater burden can we have than these *evils* we've been taught with shame to shun? No baggage that we carry could be heavier than this because we live in daily horror we might drop it. Yet that is precisely what God wants us to do – give it up! "Let go and let God" means not only giving up the outcome we most desire, but also the *feelings* about losing it.

"Ye cannot enter the kingdom of Heaven except as a little child." I've often pondered that parable. Does it mean the resurrection of our inner child that we buried to become adults?

We have the potential for 64 DNA, and have 'turned on' only 20. Do you know what turns on DNA? Emotion. Did Jesus have *on* all 64? If we were fully conscious of every single emotion, got its message and safely released it, would that moment-to-moment consciousness of every necessary emotion *turn on* our full DNA?

"And the truth shall set you free." Did Jesus mean that if we were as truthful with our feelings as we are with our words – that maybe we, too, could heal? Is that what made Him able? Are we capable of that much honesty?

Chapter 8

Love Ye One Another?

At one point in time I wanted a t-shirt that boldly read on the front "If one more person tells me to save the rainforest and doesn't tell me *HOW*, I'll scream." And I feel that way about love. Everyone wants to be deeply loved, but *how* is the eternal question. I know, for certain, this much is true: We can't receive love from other people until we first love ourselves. *That's* what's hard.

As a substitute teacher I always admired the kids that said "I don't know." Until we sincerely admit where we're lacking, how can we search for more? Are we like the adults in *The Emperor's New Clothes*, unwilling to admit the charade? We helplessly watch the world situation and the only solution our leaders can offer is to piously say "Love your neighbor"? Children kill children, violence increases and the root of the problem is hatred within, and the only advice is "Don't hate"?

Well, hello! It's not working! Have you noticed? And if someone can't find a better solution than "Come on guys, be nice!", the madness and massacres will inevitably continue while we prattle more platitudes from the pulpit.

It's bizarre to imagine that one little girl in Peoria could find an answer. But I did, and it works, and it can work for you... and everyone on the planet.

The root of most conflict, from an argument to a war, is trapped negativity within. It is not acceptable to cry and scream so we throw our rage at our enemies. They represent the *evil* that we hide (our shame of our negative feelings), and we continually do battle *out there*. Our *opponent* represents the opposing emotions that we hate inside ourselves. Our *adversary* is the adverse half that we loathe and deny within. If we would address our own inner angst, there would no longer be need to attack.

We are all interconnected – we are, in truth, One feeling body. If pressure builds up in humanity's cells, it must find a way to release. Because no other recourse was available, war has been the instrument of that purge. If we genuinely desire to bring peace to the world, I offer a choice besides battle: Daily, earnest prayer and commitment to discharge, in harmless ways, *our portion of the collective sorrow*.

Imagine – if one million people did a daily cleanse, that's one million less, in a war-torn region, that might not need to die. Instead of complaining of helplessness, bring peace to yourself – thus, the world.

Those screams I heard that infant scream don't just go away. Think about it. Think about the last time you were in the presence of rage. It's a huge amount of energy. Now, do we think that monster is fabricated by the brain, a fancy show to scare us? No. That baby was scaring the heck out of me, just by physically expressing his pain. (Remember, emotions are not mental – they're a biological change in our cells. They need to be addressed physically – not intellectually, not resolutely, not morally. Analysis comes later, after physiological release.)

So if rage – that volatile energy – is ignited by the body, not the brain, then how could my brain with a simple "decision" force it to go away?

It can't, is the bottom line answer. It never could in the past, it never will in the future and we have to quit demanding that it try. As ugly a scene as we witness when we're angry, imagine that's been festering for years. And since energy never disappears, it simply changes its form, should it shock us when it reappears in an even uglier form – cancer, disease and violence?

The most educated people have the highest rate of cancer because they are proficiently skilled at *coping*, at rationalizing the bete noire away. I enjoy that word *coping*; it's so much like copping out. When I hear phrases like "holding up well" and "not letting it get to me," or "I'm keeping my head above water", or "not letting it get me down," we're "handling, maintaining, and adjusting so well", I think of our sister in Africa who knows none of these *virtues*. Some would call it uncivilized the way she screams and groans. But I call it the highest wisdom, for she knows how to keep herself well.

I've heard about a program for abusers to help them to control their anger. It takes 26 weeks and they are taught, in a nutshell, "the fine art of mental reasoning". Oh great! Now they'll be joining us "civilized" folks and die of a heart attack. And if you've been beaten, that doesn't sound bad, but there *is* a better solution.

We have a choice: We can allow the expression of anger through war, violence, and crime. Or, we can continue to stuff our emotions till they resurface as all our diseases. Or, we can teach a safe, harmless method of defusing this destructive bomb.

For hundreds of years, in biblical times, people had been waiting for a king. They expected his arrival with a glorious army, to valiantly vanquish their foes. Imagine their surprise when the king appeared as an infant, vulnerable and weak.

Might there be some symbolism here, something that applies to our lives? Could it be that the bringer of our greatest peace is the *baby* inside of ourselves? The one that we've silenced, ignored and abandoned in order to become adults?

That infant is none other than the Christ Child who knows how to keep us well. Respect his spontaneity by allowing full expression of his wisdom. God designed a perfect body and the Christ Child will keep it whole. He'll empty your heart of the grief and the fear, the rage, the resentment and the sorrow. When the burdens are lifted and the demons are freed, what remains is **only** the love, and we can finally fully love ourselves. And others, as reflections, will love us. We've been seeking love from people around us but what's been missing is <u>our own love, denied.</u>

Remove the "eg" from negativity and what is it that we are left with? Is it possible to change the view of our passions as the "presence of the devil himself", and recognize that our unpleasant emotions are more like the Nativity? Few paradigm shifts I can imagine would be as major as this. If we could embrace our 'shameful' half, we'd become whole, even holy – and the Christ Child could be born within.

You'll discover the Earth through your re-born eyes: the wonder, the majesty, the delight. Light will appear around people and trees and you'll feel washes of bliss at a sunset.

What you've done for yourself, you've done for us all – everyone is connected. Though we appear as many faces, there is only One of us here. As one heals, it heals us all. You'll feel and follow the need in the world, not because you think you *should*, but because it's the greatest adventure of all – returning Earth to the heaven she is, as we naturally, effortlessly, joyfully, flow love to one another.

If the Earth
were only a few feet in
diameter, floating a few feet above
a field somewhere, people would come
from everywhere to marvel at it. People would
walk around it, marveling at its big pools of water,
its little pools and the water flowing between the pools.
People would marvel at the bumps on it, and the holes in it,
and they would marvel at the very thin layer of gas surrounding
it and the water suspended in the gas. The people would
marvel at all the creatures walking around the surface of the ball,
and the creatures in the water. The people would declare it
sacred because it was the only one, and they would protect
it so that it would not be hurt. The ball would be the
greatest wonder known, and people would come to
pray to it, to be healed, to gain knowledge, to know
beauty and to wonder how it could be. People
would love it, and defend it with their lives
because they would somehow know that
their lives, their own roundness, could
be nothing without it. If the
Earth were only a few
feet in diameter.

Chapter 9

In the Beginning Was the Word
"Honor the Healing Power of Nature" [1]

Some of you are thinking this is all rather interesting, but where's the science to support it? (In Rogets Thesaurus a synonym for scientific is, interestingly, the word 'sound'.) Since researching facts is not my nature (my center is found in experience), I'll lead you to the explorers who do.

I highly recommend the books and tapes of the incomparable Deepak Chopra who offers a plethora of scientific evidence that correlates emotions and health. Any doubts you may have of how thoughts affect us will be permanently erased.

Dr. Mitchell Gaynor[2] is a leading oncologist at the Strang-Cornell Cancer Prevention Center and has been using sound as a complementary therapy with remarkable results. Andrew Weil is another vanguard in the mind-body connection. His books are filled with the pure common sense and effectiveness of alternate therapies.

Johnathan Goldman[3] and Dr. John Beaulieu[4] have also written two very compre-

---

[1] Hippocrates
[2] *Sounds of Healing*
[3] *Healing Sounds*
[4] *Music and Sound in the Healing Arts*

hensive studies about the awesome potential of sound. Just a few: Sound is used to induce a rhythm in the brain, heart and lungs and balance the two halves of the brain. It is used to cleanse clogged arteries and disolve kidney stones. A self-created sound produces melatonin, the hormone that can actually slow the process of aging, strenghen our immune system and prolong sexual vitality.[5]

In most ancient cultures, the god of healing and the god of music were the same. Pythagoras, the great mathmatician, saw the universe as a vast musical instrument, creating the "music of the spheres". Since our bodies are actually a vibration (Quantum Physics), it logically follows that any permanent healing must involve vibration or sound.

We know that soldiers must break out of step when walking over a bridge — the resonance could destroy it. Could there be some research here? Could we find the resonance of a cancer cell and aim at the cell to destroy it?

I honestly believe, in the not-too-distant future, we will employ sound to cure all ills, even provide inexhaustible energy. Does that seem like the fantasy of a science fiction writer? Consider this: If the universe is infinite (Steven Hawking) and is made up of vibrations, which is energy in itself, couldn't we find the appropriate vibration to tap into that endless supply?

The psychic Edgar Cayce and the philosopher Rudolf Steiner both predicted pure tones will be used for healing before the end of this

---

[5] *The Melatonin Miracle,* Pierpaoli PhD and Regelson PhD

44

century. Nostradamus foretold the healing of cancer through pure tone by 1998. I believe that sound from an external source can be a powerful, temporary healer. But the *cause* of the cancer is still unaddressed and the disease may likely return... The pure tone the prophets had spoken about, I think, is our *trapped sound* within.

Let me explain: Health could be defined as balance – each cell of the body in a balanced state, electrical, chemical and so on. For our purposes we will focus on electric: Each cell of the body has the electric potential of about one volt. Considering we have one quadrillion cells, we're talking a lot of electricity, which occurs in the acid/base fluids.

Imagine a cell floating in a liquid of a balance of acid and base. Because everything that vibrates makes a sound, the cell is making a balanced sound, though inaudible to human ears. When an emotion washes over the cell, the liquid around the cell changes. If it's happy, the cell vibrates quickly, causing a higher pitched sound. If it's sad, the cell slows down in vibration and causes a lower pitched sound. The natural gut response to pain is to cry or to utter a moan. I think our instincts want to blow out the new sound that is vibrating too fast or too slowly.

Think about it: If Publishers Clearing House came to your door, what would you probably do? You'd scream and cry and jump up and down and possibly laugh and dance (just watch Wheel of Fortune any night of the week, because it's socially acceptable to act this way when the emotion is one of excitement.) But if the emotion is one of anger or sorrow or fear and the cell *decreases* in vibratory rate, the body wants *also* to react that way, to expel the harmful new sound.

But do we do that? No! We act strong and impervious, like it didn't hurt, but our cells know a heck of a lot better. If we don't blow out the improper vibration by instinctively releasing the sound, our cells remain in an unbalanced state, slowing down our overall metabolism (overweight) and inviting every manner of disease.

If I harm a baby or take a toy from a child, it will hit and cry and scream. If I strike a person who is mentally handicapped, they will react in much the same way. If an animal is harmed it will instinctively make noise. What are these "unintelligent souls" telling us about cellular balance? Last night I fell down, hard, on the ice, but I lay there and moaned and groaned. I wasn't making a noise, I was *allowing* the no-ease. (Our bodies' healing potential never fails to astonish me; I must have been hilarious.) But this morning I awoke and was feeling fine, bruised, but no ache in sight.

Gregg Braden[6] answers many questions and some of our ancient spiritual theories he has factually explained. He says that compassion is our natural state and there is an electromagnetic shift happening in our bodies and all life on Earth that will usher this reality in. He states that our very DNA can change by the ef-

---

[6] *Awakening to Zero Point*

fect of our emotions. We actually create new forms of amino acids by our thoughts and by our feelings. "It appears the vibratory template of emotion actually 'touches' the molecules of DNA in our cells, waking up dormant codes of immunity and vitality that may lay dormant within us." Imagine the implications! If we have a predisposition toward cancer or are branded an alcoholic for life, might releasing our trapped emotions change that?

If someone were to lead us through the confusing health care maze, out of this bewildering jungle of drugs and pills and fear, he would be an Albert Schweitzer, a Pasteur, a Jonas Salk. Few contributions will have been as great as empowering the people with their health. It won't be me, I'm just an observer, though I've experienced all that I'm claiming. But someone of a scientific mind, who can blend DNA, cells and emotion and give us the intriguing results.

Abraham Maslow was curious why some people more fully embraced life with wonder, enthusiasm and joy. Were they extraordinary people, he asked? He researched and discovered they were ordinary people with nothing taken away. Their child-likeness was still alive. The maturation process hadn't destroyed their inner child.

"I accidentally praised a tulip as one of the finest I ever saw; upon which they told me it was a common Fool's Coat. Upon that I praised a second, which it seems was but another of the same... The gentleman smiled at my ignorance. He seemed a plain honest man, and a person of good sense, had not his head been touched with that distemper which Hippocrates calls the Tulipmania; insomuch that he could talk very rationally on any subject in the world but a tulip." [7]

Whoever is the scientist that can lead us from this maze, will not be only restoring our health, but returning the wonder and awe that we lost as we embarked upon adulthood.

"The most beautiful and profound emotion we can experience is the sensation of the 'mystical'. It is the source of all true science. He to whom this emotion is a stranger, who can no longer wonder and stand rapt in awe, is as good as dead." [8]

Our emotions are our passport to mystical and spiritual growth. They are *pure energy* coming directly from God. The logical mind will desperately endeavor to deny unpleasant feelings because we've trained it from the time we were small. But the boundaries we set for our emotions become the boundaries of our spiritual experience.

Or, as another great thinker put it simply, the kingdom of heaven is within.

---

[7] Joseph Addison

[8] Albert Einstein

Chapter 10

"The Body Is a Printout of Consciousness" [1]

All matter and energy are the same thing: $E=mc^2$. Both strive to be loved because Love is their name and won't rest till enfolded in the One. Dis-ease (un-lovingness) in our Spirit must appear in the body to get our attention. Much of the energy of emotion is unloved, so *illness* is the body's way of getting us to look at it and love it.

Pain is the unwillingness to feel an emotion. Let me use an example for this: That pain in your shoulder is there because a negative sensation washed over you and you didn't love it and allow it to move, up and on out of the body, like the un-adult-erated infant before he learned to pretend.

"No, I pulled a muscle" you say.

Again, if I may, I suggest you pulled a muscle because an emotion arose within the wisdom of your cells for your own survival and you aborted it. Whenever we abort a natural flow of energy there will be consequences, and you *pulled a muscle*.

"What about a virus and disease?" you ask. Every day we're exposed to thousands of germs and the body processes them out. But if there's a need to release sound, movement and

---

[1] Deepak Chopra

tears, to look at the energies we've unlovingly repressed, we trap that germ and get *sick*.

Now I am well aware of how crazy this sounds, but let me ask you this question: Do you believe that when you die you simply no longer exist? That what you've achieved and evolved into disappears in the dust of your cells? Probably not. The vast majority of people on Earth believe in an afterlife – that we are more than the elements of corporeal self and our Spirit goes on forever. (I've been out of my body and I *know* I'm not that.) So if first we are Spirit, inhabiting a body, then ultimately, who is in charge? The body? Viewing the megalithic proportions of America's health industry, I'd say that's what most of us think.

We've forgotten our primary identity. Might it be hypocritical to say we believe in heaven, then blame our cold on a germ? If I first am my Spirit, then my Spirit chose this cold because my body is lifeless without me. Remember the last funeral you went to? Could that stiff in front of you make a choice? I don't think so. And if it would have, you can bet your bottom dollar it'd make the 10 o'clock news. We think it's crazy to suggest we choose our colds yet we vainly glorify what is basically a corpse (a body disconnected to Spirit) by giving it the credit for *getting a cold. It* can't do diddly without Spirit.

The belief that our flesh is Mission Control is in the minority on Earth. More than half the world using Eastern medicine remembers who first we are. Oriental doctors must know something we don't; their culture has far fewer of our diseases. Volumes could be written, for compared to the West, the foundation of their healing is just opposite. Their approach is from within and preventative.

For hundreds of years in China people paid their doctor when they were well. As soon as they contracted an illness, the doctor accepted no payment—he hadn't successfully done his job.

Our doctors focus on disease, the effect, rather than to teach us to prevent. But Eastern or Western, behind all our illness, is an emotion that was not expressed. We are first the Spirit, amygdala brain, the *experience*. We are Cause inhabiting a body (effect) – From Within to Without, Always – not a body that, oh by the way, has a Spirit.

Now back to getting a cold. Yes, it is deeply unconscious. No one would knowingly get the flu. But if there are lots of negative charges that have built up in your cells, how else will you flush them out? (Flue, as in chimney.) Mucous, like tears, contains toxins, so allow it to move on out. The watery eyes, the runny nose, the moaning and groaning, the vomiting – is this the sound and movement and tears that finally get to be freed?

And why do they call the flu virus *sneaky?* As soon as we get an antibiotic that kills it, it up and changes its form. Could it be because our bodies actually *need* this flu to flush all our toxins out? Could the magnificent wisdom of our body, led by Spirit, be *adapting* to guarantee a purge?

In the Chinese art of placement, Feng Shui, for a home, business or garden, the purpose is to create an environment where the energy (chi) can freely flow. For five thousand years, do you know which elements were used to accomplish this purpose? Sound, movement and flowing water – curious similarity to what I suspect are our *bodies* healing tools.

We're never going to win this "War on Disease" for two rather simple reasons. The first will be explained in a later chapter by Universal Law Three (What you Resist, Persists). The second is because dis-ease is not our enemy; it is, in fact, our best friend. It is a storage of built-up toxins that, if not released, can kill us. It's a warning that something in our lives is wrong, a red light on our dash, an alarm, and we'd better pull over and quit driving the car or we'll blow out the entire transmission.

I've spoken about cancer and heart attacks; what about other diseases? I have no proof yet but I sincerely believe that if every person with any affliction would undertake an emotional cleanse, and return to a healthy diet (Spirit – whole emotions; body – whole food, loving both halves of ourselves), they would begin to see remarkable improvement. Continue with your medicine and the instruction of your physician and add emotions as an essential assistance.

Because men are taught to be ashamed of their tears, their sorrow is stored in their breast, which causes, I think, heart attacks. Women are taught to always be nice, not raise their voice, or be combative so their anger is stored in their breast, which causes, I think, breast cancer.

I'd like to see a study done of women who have this condition, who also repress their anger. As a child, I was incapable of masking my resentment and it caused frequent battles with my mother (although I successfully repressed fear and sorrow). I realize now, looking back on that time, I instinctively blew out the rage in my breast with sound, movement and tears.

So I invite you to ask yourself: If you have been taught not to raise your voice, is your anger still laboring in your breast?

If that theory doesn't feel right to you, consider another possibility. The breast represents our nurturing, what was given and what we give to ourselves. When our behavior upset our mothers, they tapped into their own inner rage, but skilled in the art of self-control, they withdrew rather than hit.

We immediately realized our error, and regretfully sought them with remorse. But if they were still caught in that angry place no amount of persuading would affect them. Their love was withheld for interminable hours (it seemed) and we read the message as such: "When I am feeling a negative emotion, I do not deserve to be nurtured."

So all through our lives, as negativity arose, we unconsciously stopped loving ourselves. An anger here, a sadness there, so natural to the human process, aborted the flow of love (life-force) to the breast and the toll has to ultimately, be paid.

If we can learn to love every nuance of emotion and feed our bodies a healthy diet, I know with every beat of my heart that breast cancer would no longer be.

Recently on a documentary about the wives during World War I, a woman poignantly said "We were busy on the home front being brave." Soon after the declaration of peace over a half million Americans died of the flu. Her summation was more telling than she realized. It takes valuable energy to repress. And if years of toxins from unshed tears have accumulated in our cells, our bodies are helpless to fight off germs.

Now, I am not a doctor and I am not a chemist. I am not a psychologist and I am not a scientist. But I have observed from a fascinating perspective, since I held that baby in my arms. If our natural instinct for releasing pain is sound, movement and tears, why is it we only use movement?

America daily buzzes in motion, from exercise classes to dancing and yoga, aerobics, ballet and clogging. (If you can work up a sweat, even better. The sweat lodge was essential to each tribe of Native Americans—they knew it's purifying effect of flushing out stored up toxins.) And thank goodness for football weekends! The shouting and stomping and whooping that goes on releases much of the workplace stress. Movement and football are socially acceptable – screaming and crying are not. But if they're the missing pieces of a naturally spontaneous human, isn't it worth a try?

Some of you will demand more facts. And, as I implored you in the previous chapter, seek them, find them, research it for us, please – many people will need clear proof.

Until that time that the data is in, won't some of us give it a try? Can we put the word *motion* back into emotion and move all this energy out? We don't share the risks of a Copernicus or Columbus, and the rewards, I can promise from personal experience, are those in the title of this book.

"Three are the dwellings of the Son of Man and no one may come before the face of the One who knows not the angel of peace in each of the three. These are body, thoughts, and feelings." [2]

---

[2] Adapted from the Essene Gospel of Peace.

Chapter 11

Our Thoughts Create Our Reality
"Imagination Is More Important Than Knowledge" [1]

I have spoken to you of Universal Law One: "What we do comes back to us." So let's go on to Universal Law Two: "Like attracts like". All matter, including a thought, has vibration and is attracted to similar vibration. That is Quantum Physics and the foundation of Positive Thinking – that if we think and feel positive thoughts, "I have good relations with people", then that reality is drawn to us because like is attracting like. If we think and feel, (however unconsciously) "Nobody likes me", which has a vibration of its own, we will attract the very circumstances that match that vibration – people who do not like us.

Scientists have recently discovered evidence to substantiate this law. Our DNA determines how patterns of light, *matter* (atoms, viruses, people, events), arrange themselves around our body. That's because our DNA is influenced by our emotions. Of the billions we're spending on cancer research, couldn't part of it go towards this fact? With no ill feelings intended, I suspect they're not too interested since a profitable drug is not involved.

---

[1] Albert Einstein (who failed his engineering exams)

The only one to profit from emotion would be the wise patient himself.

So back to 'Like attracting Like'. This solves the age-old question of 'Which came first, the chicken or the egg?' Most people think, "I don't feel safe because of what I've experienced" (or "I am the victim of my environment"). But the truth of life is, you're creating what you experience (unsafe conditions) because you're first *thinking* "I'm unsafe." Our Thoughts Create Our Reality. We, unconsciously, are the determiners of our fate, the captains of our soul.

Do you see? Your thoughts and sensations, deeply unconscious, are creating a vibration that then must be drawn to you. Your lost job, your lost love, even your lost luggage weren't accidents. Forgive my naked candor, but there are no accidents. Everything is going along perfectly according to Universal Laws (and through the book I'll use examples for each).

- What you Put out, you get Back.
- What you're Emanating, you're Attracting.
- What we Resist, Persists.
- Attention is Energy.
- From Within to Without, Always.
- As Above, so Below. [2]

[2] Examples: (1) The heat (electromagnetic) field of a galaxy is the same shape as our personal electromagnetic field when it's achieved it's full capacity—most aura's aren't complete yet. Drunvalo Melchizedek *The Ancient Secret of the Flower of Life.* (2) "Human molecular structure is identical to that of the stars." Science Magazine

These are the secrets of the ancient ones, the sages of ages long ago. If these are the laws of physical reality (that our unconscious determines our lives) doesn't it make you want to get conscious?

If your car has an 'accident' don't waste time blaming the 'fools' out there. On a deeply unconscious level, you drew that to you to grow. Remember, *all negative events happen as opportunities to release emotion*. Happenings in life are reflections of our psyche – symbols of our unconscious mind. **All of life is a mirror; the events you see before you are *you (unconsciously)* talking to *You*.** They are your internalized feelings that want to move up and out.

If, as children, we're told that we're flawed, there's an anger and sadness inside because our soul knows that's not true. Any negative messages given to a child are not only false, they're immoral, for each has unlimited potential. We can criticize their behavior, but never criticize their soul. "You're stupid", "you're shameful" is heinous treatment of a child. "What you are *doing* is wrong," we need to be saying – not what you *are* is wrong. If we could do that for one generation, we could turn this whole planet around.

So if we believe "I'm not good enough" or "I always get hurt by people", that emotion will influence our surroundings and circumstances in life will reflect that. Because consciousness (Spirit, which becomes body) is continually striving for wholeness, we draw to us situations that will discharge that un-whole-y thinking; we have a car 'accident'. But the Chinese word for catastrophe also means opportunity. Seize this chance you've cleverly created and use it for profound transformation.

Instead of playing the pitiful victim, and slinging a few measly insults, go to your room where you can be alone and proceed to write this driver a letter. (You can forget now this fool is actually an angel revealing your innermost thoughts. He represents the tip of the iceberg of feelings you've repressed for years.)

Now this letter doesn't have to be smart or clever; it doesn't even have to make sense. Pretend that you are four years old and say anything you want. It can be outrageous or silly or insane or wild, because it's not about ideas, it's about emotions. Say things that really release the charge, the fury, the disgust, the tears, (the sadness that's hiding behind the rage). It's fine to exaggerate even a simple fender-bender; just start and see where it leads you. It's like the cartoon of the couple dining, "It's not the egg rolls, Harold. It's the last fourteen years."

You'll be astonished at the depth of the emotional cauldron that's been brewing in there for years. I mean you could hold a Super Bowl party from the width and depth of that keg!

Now keep in mind this letter is never sent. (That would harm – quiz time – who?) Oh no. This epistle is for your own delectation, to relish and savor as you wish. Read it aloud, (Pacino, eat your heart out) with Academy Award winning passion. Read it four times or a dozen each day, as long as there's genuine feeling. Because one day, "Dear Driver, you slimy face of a maggot, I'd like to set you on fire." will be cooed like a lullaby, a bedtime story, because the 'charge' will all be released, and the purpose of your 'accident' fulfilled.

Look at the root of *emergency* – emergence is something being born. Let's begin viewing our misfortunes as opportunities to transform. Metamorphosis requires a time in the dark. Few things are uglier than a pupae, but few things are more beautiful than its goal.

Chapter 12

It's Time To Allow
...or The All-Ow! Times

All difficulty in life is our friend. It is striving to make us whole. It wants us to see life from a larger perspective, to expand us and make us grow. There's so much we're capable of being, but easiness doesn't require a stretch. Taking only the comfortable road will limit our journey of life and it's the hills and potholes and tornadoes we drive through that make up the elixir of joy. If we don't experience harsh failures, we'll never appreciate success. Lincoln failed a dozen times till he arrived where he was meant to be.

"The Weight is the Way".

But we're so entrenched in good guy/bad guy, obsessing what's right/what's wrong, that we rarely unwrap its gift. Did you ever notice that many people would rather be right than happy? Some of you are still convinced that "Life out there is not safe", and I could talk metaphysics five ways from Wednesday which might make you happy, but you'd rather be right.

What do you suppose is the dreaded fear of actually being wrong – being shot and stripped and hung from a tree? You'd think so, by the desperate way that people cling to their rightness. It's part of our mistaken identity that first we are our brains and any demoting of that glorious corporal is tantamount to the highest treason.

But it is precisely that – corporal. It's neat, its amazing, but still part of the body and can't spout many fancy facts while sprouting six feet under. Spirit works in miraculous ways and is infinitely more complex. So if you believe in an afterlife, let's subjugate the brain to Spirit, because if you want help in becoming happier, you'll have to lose your attachment to *rightness*.

You see, the problem with approaching conflict by only figuring out who to blame, is that ultimately, we don't get resolution (except in an angst-filled court of law which is why there are more lawyers than ministers). We may have won the battle, but we've actually lost the war because the years of rancor during a dispute take a toll on both parties involved.

We fail miserably when we try to solve discord with only our logical mind. What's excluded from the process is *sympathy*. It's as if our feelings, in order to have value, must proceed from a logical source. Much of the time they won't, and that's OK: they come from childhood issues and the present situation is only activating the repressed emotion.

It's like the age-old problem between the sexes – women like to talk in order to blow off steam, and men feel responsible to *fix* it. Gals aren't asking for it to be fixed (they'll do it themselves or ask you later). They, healthfully, just want to discharge SMuT and it's probably not the can-opener at all.

And even when the source is logical we still leave out essential empathy. One time I saw a son say to his mother "Why did you abandon me?" And she began listing the 25 reasons she was forced to give him up for adoption. They went on endlessly, shouting and scowling, but the real problem was still unaddressed. He's hurting and so is she! She thinks because her reasons were valid that *they* should erase his wounds and she fears expression of empathy will devalue her sensible choice. It won't. Her choice was good *and* he is hurting. It's a paradox that must exist if healing is our intention.

Remember, *logic, most often, won't erase our pain, but feeling it out, will.* **All that pain wants is to be felt.** She needs to express an apology to him and he needs to feel her ache. Even when we unknowingly harm we still need to sympathize. Then they need a good hearty cry enfolded in each other's arms.

- *Listen* to what your opponent says
- *Feel* what he must be feeling
- *Work* together to find common ground, then
- *United*, resolve the conflict

When we unite our brain with our feelings in an effort to unite with another we are fulfilling a mission for God – U-Knighted.

Now other than good guy/bad guy, what about bad events? "Good events are right and bad events are wrong." But allow me to suggest a fresh way of thinking. Bad events want to serve us as much as the good ones do.

But we balk and brand them as foreigners and begin a full-scale attack. We focus all our resources on how to successfully resist. In fact, I would say, the majority of unhappiness is based on a person resisting. But welcome to Universal Law Three: "What we resist, persists." "Oh no" you groan. Stay with me – there is light at the end of this tunnel.

Let me use an example for this: Let's say you have a daughter in high school who is dating a bona-fide creep. You might have noticed this law already: The more you rant and rave and threaten, the more she's in love with the guy. What we resist, persists. And you say, "But I'm right in acting this way. I'm her mother and I know what she needs. And it isn't this ugly skinhead." You might be quite right and justified, but your rightness won't solve the problem. In fact, it makes it worse.

(Now, of course, this problem can be serious — it can indicate dating abuse. Seek professional help that explains to your daughter the signs of abusive relations. In addition to prayer and counseling, add this process to address deeper issues.)

If Mom has a *charge*, an emotional issue, that causes a strong resistance, that's a signal that a trapped emotion wants desperately to move on out. The resistance you're showing is *Big Time Stress* to keep your feelings in chains. Yet your unconscious has slyly created this pickle as an opportunity to let them out. When you hear yourself saying "Don't you dare go out there." Or what? You'll whip or disown her? Pretty strong threats to avoid a few tears, because that's really all that's happening; you're digging your heels in and scrapping like a cat to avoid a heart-breaking cry.

You see, sometime in your childhood you lost a precious dream and you never cried out those tears. So that thought and feeling are still buried in there, emanating "I lose my dreams". Enter Jobo of the Shining Skull as a catalyst to bring things to a head. (No pun intended.)

So you do some indecent discharging (involving other people –no fair). You get plenty of screaming and thrashing out, but since it's landing on your daughter, harm invariably comes back in the form of bickering and pain.

Here's how you solve the problem for yourself and, probably, for your daughter. Get time to yourself and go to your room where no one will be disturbed. Pretend you're the mom in the year's hottest movie, *Allandra the Exquisite Marries JoBo the Jerk.* Now really get into this movie – you're the star who is the mother of the bride.

Imagine the wedding. How would you feel as she puts her dress on? Will she even allow you in the room? Be there as she walks down the aisle and feel all those heartbreaking tears. This would be a mother's nightmare, so immerse yourself in the horror. Imagine them moving to another state—imagine her calling with news that he beat her—imagine the almost unthinkable worst and feel all those feelings on out. Those tears have been in there since you lost your first dream, and finally you're setting them free.

(In Egypt, students of Mystery schools were required to do what you did. They learned that if they imagined the worst and felt the feelings on out, that they wouldn't have to create it. As the psychologist Jung said, "Whatever we can't imagine [look at], we have to manifest [make happen].")

Now that you've lived the movie of experiencing whatever might possibly happen, the paradox is, it probably won't. It would have happened partly for your benefit so you'd cry out lots of tears, but since you did that already in rehearsal, you don't have to do the play!

Now that you've done what JoBo the conehead – messenger boy from yourself – wanted you to do, he can happily exit the scene. The negativity that's been released from your field has left you vibrating more positively. And because he no longer resonates with you, he'll cycle off to find more prey.

For proponents of Positive Thinking and students of Creative Visualization this must fly in the face of their beliefs. But understand this: First we feel emotion through our original brain, the amygdala, and most of it is deeply unconscious. What we're *feeling* (from childhood) though not even aware, is *firstly* what we're sending out. That's why getting what we want, with only positive thinking, so often fails to succeed. We can picture and proclaim and announce and chant and all these tools are excellent, but if the child in us *feels* lack and fear, however, as adults we think we've quelled it, that feeling can only draw lack.

So if resistance comes up, instead of lying to yourself and jumping into a barrage of pronouncements, admit that you feel a negative emotion and imagine the worst that could happen. A. You're being truthful and, B. fulfilling Law, because what we put out, we get back and what we first are communicating (from childhood issues) is feeling, feeling, feeling. Once you've released the emotional charge, continue with your highest visualizations.

Since difficulty is our good friend, let's look at the often ignored flip-side of "What you sow, you reap." Jesus said "Love thine enemies and Resist not thy enemies" because He understood Universal Laws. If everything we're putting out is coming back to us, then what we're receiving, we must have sent out, no matter how unpleasant it appears. It wouldn't have arrived on our doorstep if we hadn't first sent it out. So own it, because it's ours.

That's how we learn on this planet called Earth – send out an action and get back how it feels. If it's good, we do more — if it's bad, we desist. We hug somebody, they hug us. We give a gift, we get back a gift. We loan some money, and later when we need it, somebody will loan money to us. We are thoughtful when we park the car so there is always a parking place for us. And on and on, ad infinitum.

But if we lie or cheat or steal, and then someone steals from us, do we feel out the pain of a stolen bike, then say "This is because I stole"? And try to remember when we did just that and promise not to do it again because it hurts so badly when we're stolen from? Or admit to ourselves we'd been *thinking* for years "Life out there is not safe?" (thoughts are actions too.) Oh, no! We rant and rave and call the police and talk about suing the guy. "What is good, *I* put out. What is bad, *he* puts out." Jesus must think we're a scream!

But let's remember: "Pain carves the well that will hold all our joy." If we could stop resisting our enemies and experience what they've graciously returned – the wrong we originally sent out – they'd be the bearers of our greater joy. And yes, we'd be loving them.

The need to recognize, respect and release our feelings can be a daily and ongoing process. Each time we cleanse, we raise in vibration and expose more of our Jobo (unconscious) to purge. Expect the very best to happen, because basically, what we expect, we get.

But Positive Thinking alone won't do it – it only addresses the mental and our emotions are the original Cause. When negativity arises, own it, it's ours—what we sent out is now returning. Quit playing the blame game and flush it on out in the privacy of our own safe spaces. When the tears are out and the invectives spent, it's time to return to the positive. Don't waste any time in between. Either be happy, peaceful and expecting the best, or dissolved in the liberation of our *SMuT*. No wallowing in the middle allowed (which is depression or fatigue from slow-downed cellular rate).

Do you realize why this book is unusual, what merging of polarities it requires? On the one hand, the willingness to scream like a baby, yet aware that we're creating our own reality, so we live as the most responsible adult. Never blaming or feeling victimized, yet privately, finding time to weep. It is a marriage of opposites— a dance of highs and lows that would challenge the Pogo-stick champion.

Roller coaster is the term you could use for this lifestyle. I know, I've been doing it for years, but I'm living proof you'll survive. And this Space Mountain is the newest frontier – searching for mysticism (the source of true science) and finding where it's always been waiting; in our subtle, passionate, provocative emotions and in the space between the atoms of our body.

Chapter 13

Call a Ghost by Its Name

Natural fear is a wonderful thing – it's a gut instinct to be cautious. *Gird* in the dictionary is a *twinge* or a *pang*, a signal to heighten our senses. *Girding our loins* comes from a time when we were far more sensitive to our bodies. It comes from the solar plexus, our lower animal self, as in the image of Pan; the top half is human, our intellectual, rational, conscious, adult self, balanced by the goat bottom, the animal, feeling, unconscious, child self.

One time when I was living on the farm, a friend and her dogs came to visit. The dogs ran up to Billy, my goat, and began to bark and chase him. The goat was frightened, and I heard myself scolding, "Billy, relax, they're not going to hurt you – they only want to play." As his cries became more desperate, I got more cross with him, feeling rather embarrassed that my pet was such a wimp.

My friend and her dogs soon left and I walked out in the field to see Billy. He was still shivering and shaking, and whimpering with pitiful sounds. He'd been absolutely terrified and I'd cruelly dismissed him as a coward. I was overcome with sadness at my brutal callousness. I wrapped my arms around him and wept deeply in his fur.

I realized it was exactly what I'd done to myself all those years. I was terrified, from an instinctual place, of performing before hundreds of people. (Who isn't?) But instead of admitting and allowing it and comforting myself in the fear, I had unconsciously cruelly scolded myself for not being strong and tough. I'd made feeling vulnerable, frightened and small something to be ashamed of, as if the only value I have is when I am forceful and bold. And I realized the fierceness I'd felt toward myself, I'd manifested in the criticism of critics.

And most of us do this all day. We're ashamed of the fact that we're feeling afraid, or angry or ready to cry. But these feelings are natural, they are there to protect us, and they deserve our equal respect.

I'm sure the importance of stifling this stuff comes from a primordial memory. Thousands of years ago, as humanity evolved, survival was our supreme intent. If you were hiding behind rocks from a band of Neanderthals you sure didn't want to cry. They'd hear you and find you and hit you with a club and steal your woman and furs. To cry or be frightened was to let down your guard—to not be in control was a risk.

But if you will allow me to again be Susie Friend, the character from the play *Uncommon Women*, "Announcement! Everybody ...Announcement!" We're safe. The marauding Neanderthals are gone. We can cry now. And be frightened now and shiver and shake and whimper.

And guess what – we won't die. In fact, my considered opinion is, we very well might if we don't.

Do you think it's wimpish to break down and cry? Well, I'll tell you what I think. The hardest thing I've ever done (and I've done lots of hard things) was to finally, get in touch with my pain. In fact, I wonder if people were polled, which act of courage they'd prefer – going into battle to fight our foes or facing the 'enemy' within? (Is that why wars continue?)

Let's create a new paradigm by admitting the truth – it's *much easier* to pretend we don't hurt. We've gotten so skilled, so adept, so polished that it's effortless now, not to feel. We're on automatic, it's second nature, our Pavlovian brain does it for us. "This sensation will get me in trouble – ignore it and go on to something else." So don't tell me you're tough and strong by not dissolving in the chaos of your cries. That *strength*, that *macho*, is a sham to the people who know what real strength is.

Jesus knew how agonizing it is to open our can of worms, but he knew the rewards were unlimited. "If thy whole body... has no dark part, then the whole shall be full of light." And, "My strength is made perfect in *weakness*". *That's* when He can enter our lives. We can't "enter the kingdom" (become children of God) until we will surrender our limited identity and the foolishness that *we* are in charge.

"Melt me, mold me, fill me, use me." The words to this song, repeated, can embark you on an odyssey of surrender.

Now, other than instinctual fears, there are mental, universal fears we all have one or more of. Issues of abandonment, safety and trust, self-worth and basic survival. Now let's go back to what we said about thoughts. "If we think it, it then will result." Remember which comes first. As Thoreau said, "Most people live lives of quiet desperation" because they are thinking that what happens out there gives them cause to be afraid.

But the game plan for planet Earth is surprisingly quite the opposite. Our thoughts and emotions, our very DNA, determines the reality we see. For instance, if my subliminal fear is, "I'm not safe", then I will unconsciously expect that in my affairs with people. I will see my family as threatening. I will interpret harm in words and actions that never had been intended. And no matter how much evidence is presented, I will still condemn them as guilty. "Well, I feel unsafe," I'll say to you. "And feelings do not lie."

When we are whole and have released all our fears, it is *then* that our feelings don't lie, not until. Our mental fears corrupt the purity of our natural instinctive knowing. And if I persist in feeling unsafe, I will start to draw to me the very conditions that genuinely are unsafe. My fear is creating the world that I see—the world is not creating my fear. But because the source of my fear lies within, therein lies the source of my cure.

Here's what you do: Write down what you feel or have *experienced* about everyone you know. Be honest. Now is not the time to be forgiving, or understanding, or kind – that's what got us in this mess in the first place – we talked ourselves out of our feelings.

Forgiveness is more than saying, "I forgive you." It's releasing the sound and movement and tears that are trapped since the original wound. Look at the word *ab-solution*. If pardon is no more than a mental choice, then the physical toxins contained in the tears will stay repressed for a few more years, but they *will* get our attention. That pressure must express in some way. Will it have to be through cancer?

Then review the universal fears and scan your confession for a pattern. "Are people repeatedly harming me? I must not be feeling safe. Am I often treated with disrespect? I must have low self-esteem. All of my boyfriends eventually leave me. It must be a fear of abandonment. I never have enough money. I must fear for my survival."

Now take each fear and visualize each person whose actions, you think, have 'caused' it. Then take out the picture of yourself as a child and ask him to react to their actions. He'll know how, just leave it to him with enough supervision to be safe. If you blow out your instinctive reactions to every villain on your list, it will probably never happen again. Just to make sure, read *You Can Heal Your Life*[1] and retrain your unconscious mental tapes to dissolve any remaining doubts.

---

[1] Louise Hay

How often have we tried to *overcome* our fears, but healing can't occur if we jump *over* things — we must be willing to walk our way *through* them. It's only by aligning, accepting, and allowing, that our shadow turns into light. What we resist persists—but what we accept, transforms. So name these ghosts that have haunted you for years with clarity, purpose and conviction. Each is your ticket for transformation to an identity more wonderful than you know and all that it takes is embracement.

Now some fears are purely physical: "I'm afraid of heights, afraid of strangers, afraid of flying, afraid of dying, afraid of drowning, afraid of starving, afraid of snakes, or spiders or dogs or fire or water or pain." Then go out in a boat or a plane or a tower or in your mind's eye (which is as real as reality) and project the most frightening scene you can imagine and be willing to *feel* your way through it.

Whether the fear is mental or physical you need to release its charge – the shivering, shaking, crying, sweating, moaning, screaming, laughing, sobbing – whatever your body naturally needs to expel the pent-up charge. Allow, allow, allow it all and your loving acceptance will transform it. For every second you're feeling, you're healing, for that feeling just wanted to be felt.

Realize that behind each negative emotion is the remembrance of love being withdrawn. Today we feel bitterness, jealousy, suspicion, because the tears from childhood when we experienced that trauma of our parents withdrawing their love weren't permitted to be released. And the present event is activating that suppressed disillusionment – it wants to move on out.

So in a moment of suspicion or anger, instead of responding as the adult, "that person wants to harm me", take out your child who lives within and hold him, comfort him, hear him (the way that you would if you saw a small child cry over a disappointment). If it helps to imagine, put him beside you in a chair and listen to what he has to say. This isn't crazy—he's very much alive and hasn't been heard for too long. He isn't a silly intruder in your life—he's a healer of Promethean proportion.

The words he will speak and the tears he may shed will startle and transform you. Trust in yourself, your inner kinder and God who speaks truth through your child. "And the truth shall set you free". Together you'll create a life without fear and hopefully teach and empower this world how each of us can do the same.

Chapter 14

A Priceless Paradox

"You mean," you are thinking, "if I daily release my repressed internal baggage, the reward for that effort, among many others, is that I'll actually, finally, become rich?"

Yes, I do mean that – as rich as you want to be.

But first let me give you even better news; you are deliciously rich now. And if you want to get even richer, you only have to start *feeling* it.

The word 'aware' comes from 'waer' – cautious. Our caution comes from our instincts, our gut. To know something in our heads and be aware through our senses are two halves of a balanced life. Think and feel, head and heart, work and rest, express and impress, shine and reflect, do and be. Now if I may offer a theory on why our lives have problems, it's because we are out of balance, and I'll let you tell me where. Do you *know* anyone that rests, reflects and feels too much? Probably not, but if you do, you're lucky. Spend time with them – they have much to teach.

No, most of us are fervently bent on acquiring, achieving, accomplishing, and obtaining – superseding ourselves and the friends we compare to. But when does the pleasure come in? Do I wait till I retire? What if I don't make it? As a recent TV commercial said, "It isn't what you have that makes you happy – it's how much you enjoy what you have."

We've lost the art of enjoying, relaxing, appreciating and savoring life. Do you ever sit on that gorgeous white couch? Do you really taste that wine? Are you hearing that new CD? What we're wanting and lacking is richness of *feeling.* Matter, material, stuff, is empty – it's the *experience* we have with it that gives joy. Getting more stuff will not bring bliss, but *experiencing* what you have will.

So let's pretend you're an actor enrolled at Julliard and train yourself to feel. That's what you've been searching for in your life-long quest, but you already own what you want. Your treasure's not out there, difficult, and far – it's waiting inside your six senses.

You start by bringing your attention fully inside your body. This will not be easy because no one has ever taught us. We're in school for a minimum of thirteen years, being carefully told what to think, but no one has taught us how to feel. That was a messy, unpleasant subject, and we were punished if it ever came up. So we checked out of our bodies and into our brains where we could control those awkward outbursts. We won contests and approval notching straight "A's" on our belt and for spewing back volumes of facts.

And except for sex, a massage and a drunk, that's where we've been ever since. (Obviously the worst-case scenario, but somewhere on the continuum between that and blissful nirvana is how much we are willing to feel. And if we are truthful about where we are, that's half of the battle already.)

"But I have to go to work", you say. Fine, I say. This learning doesn't take time – it just takes a shift of awareness. You're not going to be in the past or tomorrow, you're going to be in the present – the gift that is there every second each day if we only *present* it to ourselves.

"Time is the perpetual elaboration of the absolutely new." [1]

O.K., first you wake up. Feel the bed, the warmth, the softness, the peace. Do you remember any dreams? They are your feeling nature, talking to you, so if you want, write them down. Your intuition will translate them as you gradually become more aware. Want to really enjoy your shower? Go camping for two weeks or a month. I'm serious. Fourteen days of sleeping on the cold, hard ground with three or four showers at most, will brand a memory in your skin and also your soul and no future shower will be ignored.

If you want your kids to be happy and rich, send them to Outward Bound or teach camping. They sure the heck don't need more – they need to experience *not having*. It's only through

---

[1] Henri Bergson

contrast that we appreciate the amazing bounty we have. Why so often are spoiled kids miserable? They never know what they have, because they have never known not having it.

Now taste that cup of coffee. Does it need more milk today? Feel how it ignites the switch and suddenly day has begun. Enjoy that second cup too, because soon when you're awakened to all of who you are, your increased energy won't require it. Taste the bacon, enjoying its texture. As you lighten your load of unconscious baggage, you'll want to eat more lightly. But, not because you *should*. "I've been *should* upon all my life" someone said, but because it naturally, from within, will sound good, for today, but maybe not for tomorrow.

Now climb into your comfy car, old or new, fancy or plain, you're still in the minority of people on Earth who happen to own a car. Let's get some perspective here: Remember the *Summary of the World?* If camping is too brutal a thought, remember the needy in this world and how blessed America is. As we empty our hearts of the hurt and the pain, what is left is compassion and remember them we will.

Now you get to work. Feel the better fit of that traded desk chair – smell the fancy new coffee they're trying. Give a gift to someone who's often ignored – delight in the completion of a task. Having brought something special, go outside in the sun and savor your lunch by yourself. On your break, go walking and breathe deeply, listening to the language of the birds.

After work when you stop at the grocer's for milk, buy a single rose for your spouse. For the dinner you've arranged to get everyone there, so invite Mozart too. And later that evening, when you're having a tryst, scatter rose petals over the bed.

Do you see where I'm going with this? What we want is not to feel rich. What we long for is to *richly feel*. Introduce yourself to your feeling side and listen to it all day long. You will taste the tomato and hear *Blue Suede Shoes* and smell freshly cut grass and feel your child's hand and see the red sunset. The day will have been a corner of heaven and it won't have cost you a cent.

In my favorite play *Our Town*, Emily, who has died, asks God if she can return to Earth. Her wish is granted, but she doesn't stay long because she's overwhelmed by disappointment. "Do human beings ever realize life while they live it?" she asks the stage manager. "The saints and poets maybe", he replies, "they do, some."

By beginning a process of a daily cleanse to defuse your negative emotions, you will raise the overall vibration of your cells and awaken full capacity of your senses (richly feeling). Now since like attracts like, your increased vibration will draw an increased lifestyle (rich).

As long as we are feeling lack, we are vibrating that thought "I lack", so our DNA graciously arranges before us the very situation we've been feeling – lack – and that becomes our experience. Though our feelings come first, know that our words are extremely powerful. They are edicts, decrees, pronouncements, commandments. "I am", are our two most powerful words – whatever follows will manifest. I am *sick*, I am *well*, I am *rich*, I am *poor*: Fill in the blank and watch it happen. Your word is truly your wand.

Keep in mind that manifestation requires this trinity:
1. *Do* all you can do.
2. *Pray* with sincere emotion.
3. *Feel* (believe) you have the desired result.

That's why Jesus said, "Ask for something believing that ye have it." We have to do our partnering by first *owning the feeling* of wealth, so that we can vibrationally draw it to us. We won't always get what we ask for, but we will always get what we need, because God's plan for the joy of our soul is infinitely superior to ours.

If we begin feeling and speaking with gratitude for all the abundance in our lives (which unquestionably is the truth – even the poorest family in America has far more than its global kin) that vibration goes out and draws more abundance and more and more and more. Which brings us to another Universal Law – **Attention is Energy.** If I focus my attention on how much I lack, I will energize more lacking to me. If I focus my attention on how much I have, I will draw more *having* to me. Do you see? (a fuller explanation of this in chapter 18).

The reason Meister Eckhart said, "If you only have one prayer, let it be Thank you", is that gratitude is a high vibration. Because we are all connected, when we're emanating that frequency, like a stone's ripple on a pond, it will spread through the world like a healing and return as beneficence for us. If a prayer is asking for something good, the surest way to receive it is by first putting out gratitude for what we are already blessed with.

A discussion of wealth would not be complete without addressing the issue of materialism. Our habit when we need something of buying *brand new* has a deleterious effect on the earth. Please look at the word expensive – 'ex' means without and 'pensive' means thought. America is consuming three quarters of Earth's resources to satisfy our need for 'new and shiny' which, in most cases, is our lack of self-esteem. The deeply unconscious feeling from childhood, "I don't have value as a person", often translates into surrounding ourselves with 'valuable' houses and cars.

If you claim to be a steward of our only home, I invite you to question what's motivating this drive, this disdain for something that's been used. We go to church and sing songs of unity, yet hesitate to use a brother's rake. The willingness to begin buying something of another's is the willingness to connect to our

Oneness. And the discomfort you feel as you think that thought, can start a journey toward a wealth of self-discovery, worth millions of dollars, you'll learn.

Excessive consumerism is fueled by souls that *buy* something to make themselves happy, instead of rooting the unhappiness out. They end up by 50 with all the Right Stuff (and I don't mean in terms of character) but find that the cars, the clothes and the country club haven't placated their inner child. The only thing that will reveal the happiness *we already own* inside, is to remove the stagnant blockages that inhibit our inherent joy.

Think of the last time you watched a child – if his diapers were dry and his tummy was full, he was delighted by a wooden spoon. (Instead of repeatedly saying No! to a child give him something he *can* play with. His instincts are to explore and learn and the more possibilities you expose him to, the greater his creativity and intelligence.)

We are born with all the happiness we need; children are innately content. But after years of being taught *prevention of expression* our cells have slowed down in vibration. And since well-being is no longer experienced inside we look to replace it from *out there;* money, relationships, materialism and addiction temporarily increase our vibration but the real problem is still unaddressed. We need to release the charge in our cells to restore us to our pristine state. "Ye cannot enter the kingdom of heaven except as a little child".

Native Americans understood this premise—that negativity must be looked at, not denied. Before setting up camp or building a settlement they would first clean the entire area using sound, sage and ceremony. They knew that land, like us, holds energy and they experienced the comfort from releasing it. They respectfully spoke to the contained energies and freed them to their next higher good.

Any place a battle has occurred the land is still storing the trauma. That's why Kosovo was the war torn area – during the Crusades it was the location of the entire Serbian army being destroyed. The land has never healed and because Like attracts Like, traumatic events are still drawn there.

If you want help in clearing land, read *Perelandra Garden Workbook.*[1] She recommends cleaning only your own, but visualizing an area bathed in golden light is acceptable and effective everywhere.

We've reflected on wealth experientially and metaphysically. Let's look now through the eyes of Spirit. Deepak Chopra, a wholistic MD, raised his children in a fascinating way. He told them not to worry about grades or their futures or which jobs to get. He told them each child is born with a gift, a contribution they can make to the world. He asked them only to learn what that was, what benefit they each could offer.

---

[1] Michelle Wright

They went on, of course, to get excellent grades and be accepted to the finest schools because their goal was not "What's in it for me?" but "What can I do to serve?" They discovered what they loved to do and its purpose was the improvement of others.

Affluence comes from 'fluere' meaning 'to flow', and the more we give, we get. They lived the principle of Universal Law 1 – What we do comes back to us. And doesn't that make sense? If God knows we, His hands and feet, have thousands of people to serve, don't you know He'll exceed our needs? But, if *we* are the only focus in our lives, why would He bless us with fortunes? So we can buy another Ferrari that still won't fill our emptiness?

Fancy stuff gives shallow contentment because the soul's deepest longing is to serve. When we follow, uniquely, our talent for giving, it will lead us to our joy and abundance.

Chapter 15

Give It Up

"Those who are led by the Spirit of God are children of God. When we cry, Abba, Daddy, it is His Spirit bearing witness with our spirit that we are children of God. Such knowledge is too wonderful for us; the mind cannot contain it." [1]

Twice in my life, I've had an extraordinary experience – maybe you've had one that was similar. I was twenty-five, living in New York, making plenty of money at commercials, yet overwhelmed by lost boyfriends and a tired, broken heart. (I hadn't learned yet how to release it on my own and had no roles I could do that with – selling Tide® doesn't require tears or groaning; in fact, they frown on it at auditions.)

I came home, because the pain felt like homesickness, and went out in the yard to reflect. Here I was doing the best I knew how, yet I couldn't solve my aching problems and realized that I needed help. (I had always loved God from the time I was a child, but our relationship went something like this: "You're great at sunsets, you really are – but thank you, I'll handle my life.") I, the strong, the capable, the smart, the rich kid, needed help.

---

[1] Paul in Romans 8

87

(We're so programmed to be strong and independent and to never admit our weakness, but its only from recognizing we can't do it alone that we receive the power to do it. Anything we're accomplishing without that power is a fraction of what we could do.)

So I yelled, "Help me, God!", at the top of my lungs. Instantly a delicious heat washed over my entire body. It was so comforting and tender that I fell to the ground crying, like an infant held by arms. And I wept for what seemed like hours, on the damp and listening grass. When it was over, my homesickness was gone and I realized something profound: I had returned to my true home in God by admitting I was still His *child*.

The dam had broken. The Pollyanna pretense, that I had it all together, was consumed by the fire of God. He knew of my closeted burden and, as I threw it to Him to carry, he electrified me with His catch.

It happened again twenty years later, and you're going to be shocked by the cause. I'd gotten in the habit of continually knowing what it was I felt, and I realized it was the unthinkable, the unallowable, the biggest sin imaginable – I hated God's guts.

I went out in the woods, visibly shaking because I was terrified of what might happen. But, from the last twenty years of closeness with God, I knew I had to be truthful. I pictured Jesus right in front of me, and I opened fire and let'er rip. He'd promised how great and perfect life could be if we'd give it over to God. And boy, it sure the hell wasn't. It was filled with sorrow and pain and misery and loss.

"What lies, what deception, what trickery!" I screamed. "The bargain I struck with you, hateful God, (I'll spend my life serving you in exchange for peace) has been cruelly defaulted on!"

Now you and I can easily see the flaws in my 'erroneous' anger. As adults, we understand the complexities of God and are proficient at explaining our pain away with an appropriate quote from the Bible. But God's *child*, who we are (our feelings, our cells), isn't capable of logical reasoning – it just knows it's hurting. It wisely wants to blow out the bad sound that was caused by the negative emotions. (chapter 9) It deserves our love and respect as much as our logical adult. If we are healthy and whole, we're two people – a sensitive, feeling, wonder-filled child and a sensible, reasoning adult. God loves us both, can't we?

These opposites not only can co-exist, if we're to achieve our full potential, *they must*. And the point of this entire book is that anger, however unjustified, doesn't just go away. After a stiff lecture on how determination and intellect should obliterate his improprietous existence, he'll crawl back into his cave for awhile, but expecting him to disappear defies physics. The only resolve needed is the solution (tears) in resolution.

I don't remember all the curses and threats I vomited wrathfully that day, that arose from a cavern that had silently been growing, undiscovered, for untold years. I do remember pounding the ground and weeping, "I hate you! I hate you!" When into a whimpering peace I settled, like that infant I'd held long ago, the heat, that same intense, exquisite heat, swelled over my body again. And this time my tears were of joy. I felt such love from God. I knew He loved me all the more for admitting my darkest secret.

It's not that He didn't know. He'd just felt sad that I hadn't felt safe to unveil my deepest shame. (How would you feel if your child hid that from you?)

> Can the day ever come
> when we parent like God,
> clear and pure and clean inside,
> like His son, who was true to Himself?
> To respect and to honor,
> the pain of a child,
> and ask him to give it to us?
> Not ignore and punish
> the expressing of hurt,
> but offer the arms to embrace it?
> Not withdraw and withhold now
> the love they need most,
> but welcome their dark, ugly truth?
> Can we commit to the process
> of healing ourselves,
> so they can grow in a safe, whole-ly world?

Chapter 16

Where's That Thin Chapter?

If you're anything like I was, you'd have found this chapter first. Years ago, immersed in the spiritual path, I wanted to write a book called *How to Attain Cosmic Consciousness or, More Important, Get Rid of Cellulite.* As Oprah said in her TV show on how to make a million dollars, "Yeah, but will it make our butts smaller?"

Well, here's the good news you've been waiting for: You can get thin, and you will stay thin without having to go on a diet. To jettison the baggage of a heavy heart will unquestionably lighten the load. It's not what you're eating – it's what's been eating you that's been putting on added weight.

We know that what controls the rate of burning our food is metabolism, and our metabolism is influenced by the speed at which our cells vibrate. When we experience a negative emotion, it slows down the vibration of our cells which affects our metabolism (chapter 9). Liken it to feeling happy and carefree, then suddenly hearing bad news – all of your energy disappears. Your negative emotions have slowed down your cellular activity.

Now imagine you've gone years receiving small, emotional blows. If that disruption didn't exit your body through sound, movement or tears, that depressing, heavy experience affects the overall vibration of your cells. And the result is a slower metabolism. We eat more than we are using, so it's stored in the form of fat.

When I was playing the perpetual Pollyanna, "I feel nothing but love in my heart", I battled increasing weight. At Julliard, we wore leotards all day, so I lived on cottage cheese, celery and grapefruit (except for the occasional binges of cookies that I would regurgitate then in the bathroom). But from the day that I gave up controlling my life, and emptied buckets of teardrops on God, I began to lose weight. After that epiphany, I was much more aware of my feelings and I daily release any negative emotion, allowing it to move on out. My weight is fine and remains the same, though I eat anything I want, in any quantity I want.

(Health-wise, I'm rather alarmed by the popularity of high-protein diets. If one studies Macrobiotics ("great life"), the science of balanced eating, its the unrefined grains and vegetables that create our optimum health.)

I saw a friend recently who looked very slim and asked him how he'd lost his weight. He'd gone to a person with clairvoyant sight who had told him that when he was small, his uncle had treated him abusively. My friend, being gentle and very kind, had completely blocked it from his mind. He said he began to cry. He said that for days the memories poured back and he wept like an abandoned baby. When the month had passed, he'd lost twenty pounds though his eating had remained the same.

I spoke in chapter 9 of how our sensations cause the acid/base balance to change, increasing or decreasing our cellular speed. This dynamic relation of emotion to cells determines the rate at which they vibrate. And the rate of vibration, we know, influences metabolism. If we are vibrating at a higher rate, we have a faster metabolism. If we are vibrating at a lower rate, we have a slower metabolism. And what is the factor that influences that rate? E-motion. Energy in motion.

At a very unconscious level, if we are feeling – therefore thinking – a negative, "there's something wrong with me", it causes a slower cellular vibration than if we are thinking "I'm fine". So what needs to change is not only our food, but the picture of who we are. The unconscious belief that somehow we're imperfect, which we mistakenly accepted as a child, needs to be gracefully, lovingly dissolved, along with the attending heartache.

Here's what you do to shed pounds: begin today being aware of your emotions, asking your Higher Power to help. I promise you, you'll need the assistance to dissolve a fortress of defenses. (It's often easier to cry in the morning because our dreams assist us in revealing repression and our sensations are still at the surface.) Be willing to ask yourself all through the day "What *is* it that I'm feeling?" When you notice a negative emotion, name it, then love yourself for feeling it – it is serving you in some way.

Then, finding a private space, take the photograph out of yourself as a child and give it permission to react. Make sound and movement and *go for the tears* and an energy will be released. Do it each day for present distress and also find time for past hurts. Go back in your memory to painful occasions and react the way you wanted to then.

If you're a real go-getter, go into the future for whatever you're *resisting* (chapter 12) and imagine the worst that could happen. Because we draw to us whatever we fear as a chance to release emotions, by discharging the fear prematurely, you'll not only reduce the chances of it happening but increase your fat burning metabolism. Express past, present, even future emotions, and it won't take long to lose pounds.

Now the funny thing is, the more life force that replaces the freed lower energies (of fear, anger and sorrow), the more you'll crave the life force foods – *like* frequency attracting *like* frequency. As you do your daily releasing, you can observe your metabolism accelerating by your increasing enjoyment of live foods. Occasional meat, fish, whole grains, fruits and vegetables, nuts, juices, tofu and water will please your palate far more than processed foods ever did.

If facing your issues is too scary at first, rent movies that you know will make you cry. Spend time with a friend who also wants healing and tell each other your heart-aches. Sharing safely, our deepest fears, allows sorrow to come out of hiding. Secrets make us sick – disclose them to a good friend.

Keep a journal to record the daily cleanse – they're marvelously surprising and revealing. I'm sure you've had the experience, when writing, of realizing you knew more than you thought (and felt more than you thought). Especially if it's stream of consciousness – not thinking of grammar or being correct or clever or educated or wise. The wisdom will reveal itself if you let your pen and mind wander. Seeing on paper what was trapped in your mind often ignites emotion.

Now, when we're talking about crying for losing weight, I don't mean a few timid boohoos. They're fine—it's a start. But I'm talking about the screaming and sobbing that escapes when we connect to buried trauma.

I recently came upon *Primal Scream* and it validated all of my theories. Janov's experience with hundreds of people showed that the root of all neuroses is a sound. After a dozen or more releasings of screams their lives were remarkably transformed. Sound, he reminds us, is the most forceful healer and tears are the carriers of its toxins. Movement is only the vehicle for the body to expel them both. Thank you Mr. Janov, you were years ahead of your time. Hopefully now the world is ready, so publish again, please, your book.

You've heard the phrase "My heart was pounding"? If we don't *sound off* through SM&T, that trauma will turn into pounds. Because it isn't what's going into our mouths, it's what's not coming out of our hearts.

In Indian mythology the snake was the god of evil and wisdom both. Does that tell us something profound? Look at the caduceus, which is the symbol for medicine, two snakes coiled around a staff, meeting at the top with wings. Mercury owned it and by using it, could turn anything into gold. Do we have the courage to be both those snakes? Traveling both sides, the positive and negative, the ecstasy and revulsion, the exultant and despicable? Can we accept and love both halves of ourselves and turn our souls into gold?

Are you willing to be sponged out,
    erased, cancelled, made nothing?
Are you willing to be made nothing,
    dipped into oblivion?
If not, you will never really change.

D.H. Lawrence

Chapter 17

Human Beings or Human Doings?
"The present moment is a powerful goddess."[1]

Every day from about five to seven, I have my even-ing meditation. As I fix the dinner and walk around the yard, I reflect on the day, how it went. I have two assistants to help me with this task, be-ers to help me BE. You see all day long I've done, done, done and they help me remember how to Be. (Two home brews, mixed half with water, to the horror of my German kin – it hits me too fast if it's straight.) So armed with this heady nectar from the gods ("Beer is proof God loves us and wants to see us happy".[2]) I relax in the deliciousness of being.

When I lived in LA, as LAers will do, I was eager to learn my birthchart. So I went to an astrologer, who said as I sat down, "Now I'm going to talk for two hours, and explain your chart in detail, or I could sum you all up in one word." "Oh," I said quite cautiously, "and what, might I ask, is that word?" "RELAX!", he yelled in my ear and proceeded to do my chart. So you see I've had farther to travel than most toward learning the fine art of Being. And since our profession is what we're teaching ourselves, I won't claim

---

[1] Goethe

[2] Benjamin Franklin

any rights as an expert. (Find Perry Como if you can.) I'll just tell you that my goal is set to get as good at Being as I am at Doing – that healthy balance of a happy life: Do, be, do, be, do, be, do. All day singin' that Sinatra song.

Now why do you suppose that other people aren't as interested in learning how to Be? Could it be the overriding impression that we only have value when we *do*? We like ourselves when we work, work, work, but if we wish to be still, we're lazy.

I think it goes deeper than that. I think that the need to do, do, do is to avoid the feelings within. "Let's keep moving or the TV going, so I can stay in my head where it's safe. Because as soon as it's silent and I have nothing to do, I'm back in my body where I feel all these things, and that definitely is *not* safe!"

But what a shame! The soul is self-delighting! In Sanskrit the verb for 'to be' is also the word for 'to grow'. To be alone in God's creation in the miracle of now is a wonderland waiting to unfold. Is the entrance blocked by closets and trunks, you've been scolded never to open? Well, let's have a rigorous spring cleaning!

Throw out that rusty, ancient trunk that your grandmother's grandmother handed down – "A lady never raises her voice." Fling wide the doors of that antique armoire that your grandfather's grandfather made sure you got – "Real men don't cry."

The lies we've been told have held energies hostage, fine energies which came from God – "This action will serve you and this one will not"– got stuffed in a locked cement box. Let's open the doors and the windows within and let all that energy out. It came from God and wants to return to God, surely as much as we do.

Because, once we're clean and bright inside, we're fearless and able to Be. To let down our guard, be vulnerable and open, like a child, exposed but safe. Look at that word *exposed*. When daylight is shining within and without, we no longer need to *pose*. There's nothing to hide from, there's no one to fear, because we've illuminated all of the darkness.

The wonder, the majesty and the magic within are waiting for you to discover. The TV, the radio and the VCR will take their place as our helpers, instead of the monopoly they have on our time as our primary form of entertainment. Observation of nature, of people and self will stir fascination and true creativity. Your imagination, long slumbering, will stretch and awaken and, who knows what talents you'll discover. Inspiration will find you in solitude and stillness and touch you from other realms. You'll begin living life differently, as you define who it is you are, instead of letting others define you.

The first commercial I did won a CLIO – "I look like a squirrel – who am I?" But what an adventure each of us has if we are willing to walk down that road! Do you know who you are, having discovered it on your own, or are you someone others have created?

Being is more than the state of rest; it is immersion in the *experience* of life – the revelation of your uniqueness through your senses. God made only one of you and you owe it to Him to become that. You can get to the place, like a friend of mine said, "I'm all I know this well".

Now, the other side of developing the ability to listen deeply within is the grace-filled gift we can offer to others, by listening deeply to them – to be able just to Be with people as they embark on a difficult healing. Some people will prefer to do this in the solitary confines of their home. But others will greatly benefit from the presence of your emotional support. And that means not saying anything – just extending your silent listening.

If someone begins crying, what is it that we do? We start chattering like magpies and fall over each other in a desperate attempt to stop it. We list seventeen reasons why her husband's a jerk, and why he isn't worthy of this pain. Not only do we work all day to talk ourselves out of our feelings – we're not content until we've succeeded at talking our friends out of theirs!

But that doesn't work, they just go on hold and their toxins begin a disease. So let's retrain our responses, those Neanderthal instincts into listen, listen and listen.

Tears are a holy experience; you are in the presence of God. There is nothing in the world more truthful than tears, so don't tell the criers they're lying. Bite your tongue and except for a 'yes' or 'let it out'; be still, be silent, just Be. Be in awe of the divinity of this awkward event. Very few things you could do for a friend will equal the effect of this healing.

Pronounced the other way, a tear is a 'tear' in the fabric of wholeness; it's a liquid encapsulation of our pain. Stand in wonder of our soul's remarkable ability, and honor it by giving it its due. Embrace your tears, and bless them as they warmly wet your cheeks, and they in turn will bless you.

And if you can do this for yourself and others, not resisting, not avoiding, not denying the pain, but allowing and letting it be, could this bring in the era that was spoken about, "And the lion will lie down with the lamb"? ("And a child shall lead them.")

"What soap is to the body,
tears are to the soul."
(Yiddish wisdom)

"Let it be, let it be,
there will come an answer;
let it be."
(British wisdom)

Chapter 18

There Is Nothing More to Do
There Is Only to Feel

As I said earlier, I am not a psychologist, and I do not pretend to be one. Their work is essential; if you can afford one, go. I hope nothing I've said contradicts that. No, I am just a person with an interesting theory that developed from observation and experience. (I've just put two and two together – do you get the same four I get?) In addition to your getting professional help, let me share a few random opinions.

Depression:

What's the opposite of de-pression? Expression. I think it has its cause in our cultural stigma toward experiencing negative emotions. Our cells are literally *de-pressed,* having slowed down from the storage of emotion. The sufferers have a greater awareness than most of the weight of this internal baggage, yet know of no option for dropping it. Teach them to release the tears and screams and Prozac can vanish from our shelves.

Alcoholism:

The Betty Ford Clinic has discovered that the addicts with the highest intellectual capacity most often have the lowest rate of recovery. They habitually stay in their brain where it's safe because the body holds too much pain and they've mastered the art of denial.

Because our cells slow down in vibration when we experience a negative emotion, a temporary *high* or increase of vibration can be caused by alcohol. It is said that alcoholism is in our DNA, which is irreversible, but that's not true. The most recent findings show that our DNA can be altered. By what? Emotion. We drink to run away from pain that is a charge held in our cells. If we blow out the charge, through sound, movement, and tears the cells can return to balance and possibly change our DNA.

Now that is still theory and hasn't been proven but who'd like to give it a try? The cost of rehab is prohibitive to most and this gets right to the root of the problem. We can talk forever about why we drink, but the DNA won't change. With releasing emotion, it might.

The next time we thirst (to run away from the hurt), go the opposite direction, *toward* the pain. Jump into the fire that drink would put out, and let it burn freely through, going for the tears that are behind the anger of the sorrowful hurting child that's been silenced by alcohol.

Wife abuse and battering:

This happens because men[1] feel deeply shameful about their repressed negative emotions. They've been taught that fear, sorrow and vulnerability are "wimpy, soft and weak" and men only have value when they're strong. They know they often feel these things and hate them-

---

[1] Women also can be batterers.

selves when they do; so they trap and hide these energies of *weakness* so they will never appear *unmanly*. (They weren't taught the same about anger – it's macho, forceful, and ok.)

But, because all energy must ex-press in some form, either in illness or out at the world, he discharges his rage at his *female* side by beating his female partner. He needs to be told that vulnerability is good – it's half of who he is – then taught to defuse this negative charge in harmless and private ways.

Now the woman is equally culpable – she is not a pitiful victim. She hates her shadow as much as he does and feels it should be *beaten down*. She's unconsciously thinking, "I should be punished because my parents taught me I am bad; I am a naughty person when I feel *wrong* emotions and I feel them very often, so I should *pay* for that."

His similar shame of these hated sensations draws the two of them together – like attracting like. He symbolizes her *male tough side*, the parental, authoritarian voice that wants to *batter* those emotions away. If she's taught to recognize, respect and release captive energies, she won't draw it to her again.

Drugs, gambling, any addiction:

These stem from low self-esteem and guilt from internalized *beasties*. The high of drugs and gambling is needed to relieve their persistent depression and give full reign to their sensitivity. It is a *good* feeling, so unlike the unconscious self-punishing they're inflicting. They

need to begin the process of cleansing their con-
stricting, crippling emotions. In addition to that,
through therapists or books, replacing their damaged self-image.

Migraines and headaches:

Why do you suppose that so many more
women have them than do men? I think it's because it's more socially acceptable for men to
be angry than women, and the cause of the mi-
graine is anger. I suspect these people are highly
motivated and overly self-critical. When they experience a negative emotion, it unconsciously
produces shame. The shame causes the capil-
laries to expand – "What a horrible thought, I'm
angry! I should punish myself for this." If one
were to release the anger and shame, there
would be no cause for the headache.

Racism:

I honestly believe that the root of this
problem is our fear of inner darkness. It is deeply
ingrained that many emotions are *bad* and
should be locked in a secret closet. The very
fact they are kept in the dark creates an unconscious fear. Remember, if we don't acknowledge and express, we'll have to repress, depress,
and oppress. We can't succeed at integrating
with each other until we first integrate ourselves
(make whole – unite body, mind, and spirit).

When we are as loving toward our negative signals as we are to the positive ones, we
will no longer fear the *darkness* within, which
we project on the *darkness* without. And people

will appreciate the rainbow of man and welcome each radiant hue.

Animals:

Keep in mind what I've said about healing also applies to our pets. They represent our unconscious – the respect we have toward our feelings is the respect we show to them. When people laugh and call their pets *dumb,* they value too highly their own intellect, as if instinct and body-knowledge were attributes far inferior. They're not; they're equal. In fact, consider this: If the brain is led by the heart [3], then which would you call superior?

They, like us, are first Spirit, and dis-ease in the soul will reflect in the body. That's all that illness is – a subconscious cry for change. <u>Health is happiness</u> – <u>happiness is health</u>. When we're no longer happy, we get sick. So save yourself costly veterinary bills by figuring out why Spot is unhappy. Imagine yourself living his life and experience how *he* must feel.

Animals have all the emotions we have, and probably feel them more keenly. In fact they will often "take on" our stress by mirroring our physical ailments. Begin, for yourself an emotional cleanse, so Bowser won't absorb your tension. Then figure out what will make him content and his health problems will disappear.

Would you like to live on a chain or in a cage with no exercise, interest, or companionship? I don't think so. If you can't provide Fido, daily, with these basics, then find him another

---

[3] See Nature

home. Such treatment is immoral and the harm will return to you. "Until he extends his circle of compassion to include all living things, man will not himself, find peace." [4]

Nature:

The same is true of the natural world – the degree that we need to *control* our emotions is the degree that we *control* nature. We cut down trees, chemicalize our lawn, spray pesticides and hang bug lights in an attempt to avoid discomfort. We allow developers to destroy the wilderness for acres of malls and cement because, somewhere in our technological rush, we mistakenly saw that as progress.

Maybe we can trace it back to the land rush of the 1800s. We'd never imagined such vast tracts of land that we could 'conquer, tame and settle'. But that conquest we envisioned symbolized our own inner chaos. We strove to impose *order* out there because we loathed our *inner disorder*.

One hundred years later, much wilderness destroyed, we are still not the conquering heroes, for the *wildness* within still threatens. How much more of God's precious Earth are we going to savage and enflame before we wake up to the obvious fact:

Destroying nature won't destroy our emotions, however much we try. Treating them as the enemy that needs punishment and subjugation is causing the wanton devastation of

---

[4] Albert Schweitzer

the Earth, at a time when its survival is precarious. (Gaia, in truth, will do just fine—it's *we* that are the endangered species.)

"The first rule of intelligent tinkering is remembering to save all the parts."[5]

Of all frequencies (vibrational speeds of matter) that we know of, do you know what frequency is most similar to the rate of the human heart? The frequency of the Earth! Now get this: the vibrations of a human cell are entrained (directed) by the brain. What directs the brain? We live our lives as if it's in charge, but the brain is directed by the heart. And the heart is directed by the Earth. And the Earth is directed by the sun, and the sun is directed by the Great Central Sun.

Brain (Son) led by Heart
Heart (Holy Spirit) led by Earth
Earth (Mother) led by Sun
Sun (Father) led by Great Sun (God)

Quite a family, don't you think? And if our desire is to keep us all going, we'd best shift the adulation we shower on the brain to the members more worthy of the glory.

Suicide:

If someone you know is severely depressed, get to them with this information. They are stuck in a corner and see no way out. Tell them that their fear and sorrow and anger and

---

[5] Aldo Leopold

pain are normal, that you have them too. So does everyone. They're a natural, essential part of life. Tell them you are going to stay by them and help them let it out. Be there with them as they take their first steps, hesitant, confused, terrified. Your silent presence will give them assurance, the safety to let down their guard. Listen, listen and listen some more; this is not a time for words.

When they understand the importance of discharging, make sure they get professional help, the kind that will encourage release, not someone who treats from the intellect. I recommend giving them *Primal Scream* or introducing them to *Holotropic Breathwork*.

Prisons:

Can you imagine the reformation that could occur, if we took this information to our prisoners? Criminals are there because they've never had the option of safely discharging their rage. This simple, effective process could be taught all over the globe. And when they are released, return is greatly minimized, for the cause of their violence is gone.

Violent Children:

As with illness or any adversity in life, it's far better to be preventative (treat the cause) than to struggle too late with its effects. Metal detectors and security guards are the poorest solution to violence because Attention is Energy – what we focus on we increase. Talking, thinking and worrying about violence only compounds the problem. So let's name the cause and focus our attention on effective, permanent solutions.

Young people today are more sensitive, less willing to live Pollyana lies. When you're told not to cry, be vulnerable or scared, which is half of our emotional spectrum, anger is the *single* release for the bottled up energy and toxins. (Remember – emotions are not mental – they're a physical change in our cells.)

Create after-school programs led by counselors or teachers that are sympathetic to students' needs. Encourage expression, truth-telling, admitting, in small groups or one on one. Young folks are eager to learn a safe way to acknowledge and release what they feel.

In the public schools I had wonderful success by listening to students' feelings. I told them something they'd never heard – "It's OK to be angry or sad. If somebody had treated me that way, I'd have been angry too." In other words, "You're right, that action would cause that feeling, so you make good sense to me." By showing respect for their brains and their hearts, I soon earned their confidence and trust.

Then I'd tell them why it's so important not to throw their anger at others. "Everything we'll ever do, will always come back to us" and I fully elaborate. Their eyes get big as saucers as the full import of that sinks in. If you only teach a child one thing, teach him accountability.

Then I'd explain to them the process in this book – that it takes much more courage to feel our emotions than to pretend that we do not have them. Kids, that were flunking, got better grades and joined basketball and drama club.

So often beneath the most troublesome child is an artist waiting to unfold. Their feelings are fully alive, on the surface, and an insult can cut to the bone. That's why they're often so violent – they're incapable of masking their emotions. If we can teach them to respect their sensitivity and release it in harmless ways, a generation of potential prisoners will flower into the artists they are.

From the time a child is born, he needs to know that emotions are good. That, as parents, you respect all of them – both your own and those of your child – and are willing to openly discuss them. When parents don't talk about feelings, their emotions remain repressed – causing distance, coolness and tension. They disengage for safety's sake because, they know of no recourse for these taboos. Or they regularly erupt in arguments and shouting, as a way of discharging their steam.

As parents, when we share with children, briefly, our sadness and fears[5], they will see we're not pretending to be perfect, and that they don't have to be either. Let's quit saying "Don't feel certain things", and change it to "Tell me your feelings". Create a household where no emotions are shameful and, teach how to safely discharge. The only shame involved with feelings is using them to harm another.

---

[5] But, not so much that it's burdensome.

Schools:

Have you been in a school recently? Most windows are bricked up, and water fountains rarely work, because soda is available in the hall all day, along with every snack and candy imaginable. The breakfast is a sweet roll, lunch is pizza, the classroom is filled with electricity from computers and the lighting is painfully fluorescent (which is combative to our electromagnetic field). Students heads are bent over in uncomfortable desks, with little circulation of air. The children are deprived of oxygen, water, real food and sunshine, and we wonder why learning and discipline are rapidly diminishing.

Because I'm overly sensitive, my reaction to the environment was repulsion, but for people who cannot feel it, the effect is still deleterious.[6] If your school can afford only one change, replace fluorescence with full-spectrum lighting and watch the children settle down. (In England, they used it as an experiment and discovered that performance, concentration, memory and attention span all increased remarkably and the frequency of colds decreased.)

The reason I think American kids are exhibiting a *dumbing down* (besides the detrimental affects of the classroom), is that quality is forsaken for quantity. Instead of creatively teaching in ways which make information relevant, we're amping up the amount – as if the accumulation of facts is equivalent to intelligence. It's quite the opposite. Education should aim for wisdom – the ability to

---

[6] See Sunshine in chapter 19

apply the facts one has garnered to the improvement of one's life.

School should teach children *how* to think, not *what*, for goodness sake. If individuality and creativity are not fostered, we're no better than a computer. The present era is the Information Age because we can access any fact we want. We needn't waste time stuffing volumes in our brain – it is built for far finer things. What sets us apart from our electric encyclopedia is the ability to *experience* life. Man should no longer be valued for his facts, but his ability to morally *apply* them. Isn't that what we should be teaching?

Nightmares:

Bad dreams are caused by violent feelings that have not been allowed to escape. If you teach children, and adults as well, how to recognize, respect, and safely discharge, nightmares will lessen and disappear.

Extramarital Affairs:

If in a relationship and attracted to someone else, don't have an affair – do this: Realize that it isn't the person you want, it's the *feeling* that person makes you feel. After the bloom of falling in love, we often communicate less with our mate. Children and jobs compete for our attention, and our needs go unfulfilled.

When someone makes us feel loved again, it's that feeling we want to unite with. See the person you are attracted to as an angel of mercy from God. They are, and it will be easier to remember the attraction is not about sex.

Realize the job of meeting your needs is up to you and your significant other. We usually assume that relationship will meet our needs, but often we don't know what they are. This angel appears to graciously remind you that something is missing in life. Write down with as much detail as possible how this *mirror of you* makes you feel and what you love about him. Then go to your partner and tell him your needs, along with the willingness to reciprocate.

There are so many wonderful books out there that can help in solving these problems. Or go to a therapist, or counselor or friend or discover a supportive church group. Trying to repair a relationship without God is like canoeing without a paddle. Give yourself some power. (The relationship may indeed be over, but make sure it's for the right reasons.)

Also, don't end a relationship because "he (or she) makes me unhappy" or you'll create the same scene next time. The root of unhappiness is first inside you; your partner is only reflecting what you are unwilling to look at in yourself. *From within to without, always.* In fact, for any adversity in life ask, "What, within me, am I ignoring?"

Living Singly:

The qualities we think we don't have in ourselves, we look for in a mate. The union, however, will be temporary, or eventually unfulfilling, because our Spirit strives for wholeness (holiness) and longs to achieve it within oneself.

Suggestion: make a list of the qualities you want in a mate. *Successful, attractive, sensitive, affectionate.* Now let me offer a new way of thinking. Instead of a search to find Mr./Ms. Right, begin finding these qualities in yourself. Are you as successful, attractive and sensitive as you know you can fully be? Start developing these attributes within and you'll notice that your next date has them too.

The core of most attractions is love but we're *needing* someone to love us because we're not able to love ourselves. The paradox is, as long as we don't, we can't draw someone to love us. Life is a mirror – we can only draw to us that which we already are. So embrace your whole self – every emotion included – and over time, Lover Right will arrive.

Symbolically, all sexual relations are about divine union within – a marriage of both our natures – male/female, thinking/feeling, doing/being, adult/child. The reason one is lonely and craves companionship in another is that half of one's self is ignored. The missing union is not a fairytale romance; it's our abandoned inner child.

When we pledge to love and honor our tender, hurting self – the child of Mother-Father God – the emptiness and loneliness will vanish with the tears, and we'll treasure our solitude and silence. Instead of looking to another for fulfillment, we will find it in God and ourselves. Our completeness then draws a partner who also is complete (like attracts like) – our long-awaited soul-mate.

TV News:

Just be aware, when you're watching the network news, it could win an Academy Award. The drama, sensationalism, terrors, travails, the trumpets, the drumbeats, the horror – each day's half-hour production of the *news* could rival an action-packed thriller. My favorite was the graduating class that was entering "what passes as this world". Who assigned them God?

Begin seeing the subtle manipulation, convincing you, you're not safe. "Americans are increasingly........" fill in the blank, "worried, concerned, frightened, uncertain." How do they know, did they poll us? No. They're just hoping we are so they can get us hooked, and we'll need our daily fear-fix. If there were truth in advertising, it should be titled *The 5:00 Sensational News* because they rarely tell us the good, the fine, the inspiring events that occurred.

Yes, bad news sells because they've hooked us on fear, like tobacco or gambling or drugs. But, if they had any sense of morality, they could un-hook us with good news. The problem with their greed is that many fine folks actually fall for such hype. They buy into the phony picture that the world's going to hell in a hand-basket. Nice, sensible, lovely people will believe the yarn they're spinning – that the world is a treacherous place.

But the only reason you'd have to be frightened is if you'd sent out bad stuff. That doesn't mean just bad behavior; it also means *expecting* the bad. If you think long enough, "I'll be stolen from", of course things will disappear, because, what you put out you get back, including *thoughts*, however unconscious.

And if you repeatedly watch the news you *do* begin feeling afraid, which you then will have to draw to you and the problem compounds itself. So avoid the news and begin to get conscious, becoming aware of your thoughts.

If plumbing the depths of your psyche seems daunting, do it the easy way. Whenever an adverse condition arises, be willing to answer this question: Did I *think* this into reality? Then, truthfully admit how many times you had expected something bad. *We draw to us what we fear.*

Know enough of the news to keep abreast of serious events in the world so you can assist with prayer and action. Fear doesn't help; it destroys.

The best way to aid the world situation is to begin making peace with yourself. Daily honoring your inner child, who doesn't cancel his feelings with logic, will restore the love you should feel for yourself and bring peace that passeth understanding. And because we're linked through the Spirit we first are, that peace will spread through the world.

Another avenue of assistance is the tool of visualization. Sketch an outline of the area at war and color it with a gold or yellow crayon. Post it where it will often be seen and picture the area immersed in light, the highest, healing vibration. And pray for restoration of peace and guidance for all parties involved. Pray also for the TV charlatans who lead us in the mistaken belief that war is an inevitability. They will be held accountable for fabricating a destructive lie.

Let me explain, with another Universal Law, why watching the news can be harmful. *Attention* (at-tension) *is energy.* Whatever you give your attention to, you feed and energize. If you have a cyst and think about it often, you can bet, it's gonna grow. If you hate crime and spend hours each day campaigning against its existence, the chances of you being the *victim* of one have exponentially increased.

What you resist, persists. Your thoughts create reality. What you think about, you draw to you. These are different ways of saying, "What we put out we get back."

You see, the unconscious doesn't understand the word "No". It just feels the vibration of crime, so it draws more of that to you. "Resist not thine enemies" is a metaphysical truth – it never will work to resist. We must think and feel the most positive thoughts, to energize the opposite of bad – make the good so strong and invincible, that the bad dies from neglect.

Never attack behavior unless you are being physically assaulted. It's better to figure out why it's happening, and resolve it at its cause.[7]

Realize that when you express a thought like "people today are immoral," you are feeding that reality. Better to think things are fine and improving, and work to make them so. Positive thinking isn't playing the ostrich, or like I did,

---

[7] See chapter 20.

Pollyanna. It's being aware of the problems before us, and focusing our thoughts on solutions, without attacking the obvious flaws. Or, put very simply, "Do not correct the bad; instead, make the good increase."

That's why the news is so harmful – we increase the picture of doom it creates by feeding it our attention. We feed what we're watching, or saying or hearing, so avoid pessimistic conversations. Try, if you're bold, to inject optimism, but the cynics will see it as naive. Negative people cling hard to their crosses, and prefer to be right more than happy; better to find new friends.

As Paul said, "Finally, Beloved, whatever is true, honorable, just and pure, lovely and of good report: if there be virtue and if there be any praise, think about these things."

My niece, Jaymie Simmon, is writing and producing a TV show of good news. She got tired of the media's focus on the dismal direction of life. So, in Bourbonnais, Illinois, she gathered the funding to produce a beacon of light. Each show is about a community event, or person doing wonderful things. Couldn't more of us take up the flame?

Don't you suppose that the businesses in town would be much more eager to help if they knew that people were watching? If generosity was more often publicly applauded, don't you suppose it would increase? Instead of complaining about the state of the world, remember *we are the world*.

Everyone out there is a reflection of ourselves; as we serve them, we serve ourselves. So start today making a call, offering an idea to a business. The journey begins with a single step and there are few things on Earth more rewarding, than the willingness to make good news.

Well, those are a few ideas I've formed with a fresh view on how to heal. I hope you don't think that my opinions on wellness in any way preclude God. First and foremost for any healing, is a genuine connection with the Divine. Scientific data is daily coming in on the factual success of prayer. People who don't even know they are prayed for experience an improvement in health. It's now being taught in medical schools, that doctors should acknowledge its power.

This book, I offer as a catalyst to deepen our communion with God, to not be afraid or ashamed of the truth, ...to establish real intimacy with our Creator. Because the relationship we had with our parents becomes our relationship to God, this is difficult for many to do. A harsh, critical, punishing parent we (unconsciously) project on the face of God (authority). So change that perception by visualizing God as the most loving presence you can imagine.

I realize this book could be taken as a denigration of the logical mind. Forgive me; not at all. America's ability to climb out of its body and into its brain is awesome. It's one of the reasons we are leaders of the world, and our military is the finest. We've won almost every war, because of God, our intelligence and our courage. When you realize we began as frightened, shivering cavemen, shrinking in terror from our foe, to the Gulf War victory with so little human loss – what a staggering evolution is man.

Think of the gene pool that started this nation. It wasn't cheap to get on the *Mayflower*, and it sure the heck wasn't for cowards. Imagine the courage – in those years of migration – to pack a small bag with all your belongings, walk away from your village and all that you know, pay money you've saved from years of hard work to get on a dangerous, uncomfortable boat, then land in a place where you know no one, you don't speak the language and your money's almost gone. That's courage! That magnificent, applaudable ability to silence the cry of fear is boldly, supremely American and deserves our highest respect.

No, this book is not about the denigration of anything; it is about restoring a balance. The fact that America leads the world in cancer and heart disease should be a clue that our marvelous ability to ignore what we feel has gone too far. Being weak, being vulnerable, deeply feeling our pain does not mean we are not also strong. There's a time to be strong and a time to be weak; both of them demand our honor.

Can we continue our evolution of courage and take it to its finest heights? We've braved the fronts of Antetum and Verdun, the jungles of Dien Ben Phu. Do we have it in us for one last charge? It could well be the final battle cry. Can we take up our arms and go within, shine light on the enemy in the dark? The war will be ugly, full of pain and hate, but this foe never wanted to kill you; he just wanted to run away. And once you've released every prisoner of war you can name yourself among the bravest.

Chapter 19

Happy Travails to You!

I think of life as an amusement park, where each role is a ride to God. The first booth is titled *Creating a Family, Beautiful, Happy and Whole,* where people are lined up smiling. The next booth is *Having a Successful Career, Satisfying, Fulfilling, Rewarding.* It, too, is full of eager participants. Another one is named *Joining a Monastery or Nunnery to Find True Peace Within* and many folks are peacefully waiting. The next *is Making a Contribution through Science, Technology or the Arts* and it also is full.

And over in the corner is a shabby, neglected sign, *Crying and Screaming, Kicking and Moaning and Sobbing for Twenty Years.* I eagerly run up (unaware of the fact that no one else is in line) and breathlessly declare, "Wow, gimme two tickets – just in case I lose one!"

I call this ride the *Express Train* – expressing all those bugaboos out. But if it's too rapid and intense for your taste, you'll be glad there are other options, many more pleasurable to do.

Massage:

Touch is powerful tool – it brings awareness into our bodies. When someone is working on a place that hurts, that's the energy of emotion that's been trapped. Let yourself express with *S. M. or T.* and the pain, you'll find, will disappear.

Women often hold stress in their shoulders (the left one particularly, which represents our mother and female side) and perhaps that is because the relationship with her is more stressful than with father. Men often store it in their lower backs; perhaps unconsciously they feel, as providers, they must stay upright and strong and not bend with sorrow or fear.

If someone you know is anorexic, give them the gift of massage. Touch will help them more clearly feel the gaunt definition of their bodies. When they look in the mirror, they actually see fat and touch helps them feel the truth.

Deep Bodywork:

This is *not* pleasurable but can work miracles. If it's difficult for you to scream and cry, a body-worker can force them out. You just have to be willing to feel pain. You *won't* die if you go into the pain; the chances are greater if you don't. Sound, I believe, is the root of all disease and by releasing the sound held in our cells we can restore them to healthy balance. [1]

Rolfing and practitioners of myofascial release are skilled at finding our trigger points. In one hour of body work, I discharged the amount that previously had taken me months.

But if there's only a massage therapist in your area, ask him to locate your places of pain.

---

[1] Chapter 9

And instead of retreating, have him put pressure, deep pressure, as much as you can stand (using an elbow they can lean into the spot). And the key is to *keep breathing and with every breath make sound,* any sound that wants to escape. That's what the pain is – trapped sound – and allowing the noise releases the pain and the attending emotional trauma that has slowed down the vibration of your cells.

"Your issues are in your tissues." [2]

Again I recommend the work of Christine and Stanislav Grof with their research in *Holotropic Breathwork.* In a safely controlled environment, using music and deep breathing, they've discovered that people relive buried trauma and discharge resulting sound and tears.

For holotropic breathwork therapy in your area, log onto the Internet. Even if you have to travel a distance, I assure you it's worth your time.

Role playing:

Sometimes when it's difficult to access our cavern of SMuT, becoming someone else makes it easier. With a friend or group, write down on papers every emotion you can think of and have all participants draw one. Then imagine a situation and improvise whatever might happen, each person expressing that emotion.

Pick circumstances you each can relate to, and take turns playing each role. Not an emotion exists, from confusion to outrage, that we shouldn't be able to feel.

---

[2] Atsmaout Perlstein, Ph.D.

Not only will this release pent-up charges; it increases our daily awareness of what we are continually experiencing, not what we're thinking, but *feeling*.

If you're among good friends, in a supportive way, you can question their believability. "Come on, I know you can do better than that", or a pointed "I don't believe you" if the emotion is superficial. You'll discover why more people don't audition for local theatre. Getting to the heart of the electricity behind emotion is not something we grew up with.

In fact, we earned love for it's opposite. The more narrow our repertoire of emotional expression, the more patted and praised we were. But a group of friends committed to healing can encourage the quest for truth.

Music:

We've only scratched the surface of music's enormous potential for healing. In an Eastern hospital, studies were done of playing live harp music to babies. Their recovery rate was remarkable. When they played harp music that had been recorded, it's benefits were vastly reduced. It was the presence of the living vibration, so sing or play with an instrument. You don't have to be a professional to receive the blessings of tonal harmony.

But don't be discouraged from enjoying your CD; recorded music acts as geometry and works magic on our brains. "The Mozart effect" is the recent discovery that classical music improves our thinking. A field of corn grows faster and larger with harmonic, classical sounds. Conversely, discordance and broken sounds cause retardation of plant growth. In a study of fetal responses, Mozart and Vivaldi caused heart rates to stabilize and reduced the amount of kicking, whereas rock music "drove most fetuses to distraction so that they kicked violently".[3]

Singing:

Use songs you know – or make them up – whenever the situation allows. This winsome creating not only helps you feel, the resonance *tones up* your body. When we sing, we open the door to our child and the flow of spontaneous play. Make it your goal – which is possible through cleanse – to find employment that brings you joy. God doesn't work – He plays. "Creation is a game where you forget yourself."

Toning:

I highly recommend a short, powerful book, *Toning* by Laurel Elizabeth Keyes. She recounts the many benefits derived from daily vocalizing a tone. That's what I believe pain to be – the improper vibration (sound) that the cells began making when a negative emotion slowed them down. By daily toning a sound that feels comfortable, we can release that improper vibration.

Dancing:

Put your favorite music on, if possible, one with no words (they throw us into our thinking

---

[3] Dr. Thomas Verny, *The Secret Life of the Unborn Child*

brain and we want to be in the feeling). Now move ala Isadora Duncan – freely, wildly, comically, dramatically – any way your body dictates; let *it* be in the lead. Go to the place where the pain is, and allow the noise to come out. Work in that position until the noise is done.

Pain can be a cellular contraction and, if you can't get a frequent massage, release it through allowing sound. Drop your head back on your neck – if it hurts then open your mouth and allow the sound to come out. When you're straining, laboring or stretching, let the sound that wants to, escape. Imagine the healing in our exercise classes if sound was encouraged with the movement.

Laughter:

What is the opposite of gravity? Levity. If you want to break free from earth's force field (zero magnetics – bliss), spend lots of time in it's opposite. Using the same muscles as crying, the sound, movement and occasional tears cause release of stagnant energy. I'm concerned about those people who eruditely say "I never watch TV – it's so mindless". That's fine, if you want to eschew the tube, but I hope you're finding some way to be mindless or your body will demand equal time and it usually does it through illness.

Many people censor their laughter – as if it should only cross their lips if it's adult, sophisticated and complex. But our bodies need laughter and crying equally whether we *should* or not. If you can live what I've called the *roller coaster* lifestyle (when you're not laughing you're dissolved in tears, spending little time in between), it won't take long to break free. The classic Greek masks of comedy and tragedy symbolize both tools of liberation.

Suggestions: In addition to an emotional shower, add a dose of merriment each day. Rent a funny movie or tune into your favorite sit-com. Get joke books from the library and tell them at work and over dinner. Instead of watching TV every night, put on music and play *Go Fish*. Or listen to *Prairie Home Companion* on National Public Radio. Sing barbershop quartet, play *Hide the Muffin*, or put on a funny hat and dance in a goofy way. Be willing to play the fool.

It's a pitiful state we find ourselves in, if we cannot laugh at ourselves. (Studies reveal that an average kindergartner laughs up to 300 times a day – an adult averaged 17.) Encourage your children to develop their gifts, and have a weekly talent show.

We've lost the ability to entertain ourselves, but that can easily be restored, and laughter will come from a very deep place and those evenings will be golden in our memory. (Want to learn a small clue on how to look deeply into the soul and psyche of someone? Ask them the funniest thing they've heard, or what is their favorite joke? *They* are the person within the humor, and find healing on every retelling.)

Before spending big bucks for self-help speakers, ask yourself "Do they often smile?" That may seem simplistic but, whatever they're selling – if it works – should show in their face. I know for me, I've always sought wisdom from faces that were quick to smile. "God lives in a smile – it shows mastery over matter". The ultimate truth of this infinite universe (cosmic) is revealed when we drop the *s*.

I heartily recommend returning our lives to the natural elements of health:

Fresh, wholesome food:
Here's something that seems odd: they don't recommend shelled corn for humans yet we freely feed it to our birds and squirrels and even our livestock and poultry which we then enjoy for dinner. (Does that seem funny to you?) Try to eat as purely as possible with foods that are fresh and whole. But if the corner burger joint is all that time will allow, don't worry.

The state in which you eat your meal is as important as the food. If a sprout and tofu salad is swallowed with anger and ignored, that's more destructive than a burger and fries savored and relished with love. We've forgotten the purpose of eating: to connect us back to God, life force, Great Spirit. It's a thrice-a-day reminder of His gift of life and our gratitude and dependence on our Creator.

Even if it's a chili dog on the run, make eating a holy event. Thank, relax, taste, enjoy and thank sincerely again. Three times a day, connecting with Source, might gradually increase into constancy and that is the food's highest hope.

Learn all you can about nutrition. There's a book that should be in every household: *Prescription for Nutritional Healing* by James and Phyllis Balch. It offers remedies using supplements and herbs for every malady known. It will just be a matter of time before their effectiveness is clinically proven. Doctors, bless their dedicated souls, learn little about nutrition in school, so expand the wisdom they offer you with some homework of your own. Benjamin Franklin said long ago "The medicine of the future will be our food."

Clean Drinking Water:

No chlorine or fluoride. According to Dr. Kurt Donsbach, in his book *Oxygen, Oxygen,* fluoride slows down the process of burning food (oxidation) and decreases as much as 40% the necessary ATP cells in which the body stores energy.

It's a poison to destroy tooth bacteria; what else could it be destroying? It's ok for your toothbrush but leave it there. (I know this issue is controversial so let me add another dimension: When I drink fluoridation, as compared to clean, I clearly experience it as *dead*. Test your sensitivity to both and decide for yourself from experience.) Drink plenty of pure, clean water – emotions are electrical and need it to flush on out.

Sugar and coffee:

...are like drugs, for which the body builds a dependence. They block the production of joy-giving endorphins so they actually are depressants. Occasionally a desire for them is natural and enjoyable, but if you find you need lots each day, you may want to break the habit.

Black tea is one-twentieth as strong, yet serves as an effective stimulant. So does green tea, which contains antioxidants that help boost our immune system. If you can go a week or two replacing coffee with decaf or tea, and satisfy your sugar craving with natural fruits and juices, you will lose your addiction to both.

Lots of Sunshine:

Avoid fluorescent lights if you can, they wreak havoc on our electro-magnetic field (aura). A mouse's tail after four months of exposure is not a pretty sight – imagine what it's doing to us. John Ott's studies [4] show that plant and animal development are damaged by unnatural lighting. Even viewing light through glasses or a window cuts out the full spectrum of rays (though plastic retains 95%).

Couldn't we have more research? Until that time, be aware of the adversity and give yourself pure sunlight. Take lamps with full spectrum lighting to work and see how much better you feel. At least be aware of how lights are affecting you and work with them until you're comfortable.

Breath:

As suggested earlier, we habitually breathe in a shallow manner to repress our un-

----

[4] *Health & Light*

wanted emotions. This results in overweight and disease and assimilation of very little oxygen, which is essential for the body's healing. Write **Breathe** on your fridge or your desk to remind you to breathe throughout the day. It will connect you to your feelings, energize and flush out toxins. What an amazing, undervalued resource!

Sleep:

All day long our electro-magnetic field is bombarded by electrical appliances. Sleeping should allow the necessary opportunity to give our aura a rest. Make sure appliances (computer, VCR, TV, radio, alarm) are three arm lengths away. I know this sounds like it's expecting too much, but try it – you'll feel the peacefulness. A battery-operated clock at your bedside and an alarm across the room will definitely wake you up!

Cotton, Silk and Wool:

If you can, wear natural fabrics. After years of heightening my senses, when I put on even a polyester blend, I feel in two minutes, very bad. You see, we breathe not only through our nose and mouth, but through every pore in our skin. If you're limiting your breathing to only your nose, you'll take in much less oxygen. At least make sure that babies and children have pajamas with natural fabric. The building of their muscles and bones requires an optimal flow of oxygen.[5]

---

[5] It might also decrease incidents of SIDS – Sudden Infant Death Syndrome.

Walking Shoeless and Gardening:

Anything that causes us to go within is a form of insightful meditation and walking is an ideal exercise. The relaxing rhythm of both halves of the body taps into our unconscious sensing and invites hidden issues to appear.

About ten years ago, on Christmas Eve, I felt energy rush up my legs and ever since then I am able to feel the magnetic energy of the Earth. It's a very pleasant sensation of being *plugged* in to something when I'm barefoot or in leather-bottom shoes. In yoga we learn of chakras, the body's energy centers, and it's the lower ones, the belly and heart, where we store many negative feelings. Because the frequency of the earth is most similar to the frequency of the human heart, walking barefoot will open our heart and the lower blocked chakras as well.

I strongly suggest getting leather bottomed moccasins and indulging in a daily, whole-ing stroll. Our feet are our roots, that part that connects, and we do draw nourishment from the soil. They are our paws, our claws, our plug-in to the Earth and the healing vibration that it offers.

Getting your hands in the purifying soil does just that – it cleans. The Earth and fire and water and air, all are ancient purifiers. The plants, the trees, all the natural world absorbs our emotional static. So do our pets. So give yourself a daily dose, foot bared or leather-bottomed, of cleansing, purging, stress-reducing Earth and plant trees for your great-grandchildren. They're the skin, the planet's breathing pores, and in terms of its survival, are infinitely more important than we are. (The fact that a tree shares 90% of the same DNA we have should deflate some of our supremacy.)

Terra Firma doesn't need us at all; the majority of our relating to her has been anything but kind. But have you noticed, we kinda need her? Let's begin acting that way.

Be willing to give 10% of your garden to the creatures that were here before we were. If you go on a rampage against slugs on your hostas, which Universal Law will kick in? You got it – What you resist, persists. And your precious Sum and Substance will be the favorite buffet of every neighboring slug and his cousin. So give them their due, they belong here to, and the harmony in your garden will be real. In other words, Behave as if the God in all Life Mattered.

Now keep in mind, I was reared in Peoria and am aware you are probably thinking "These rides are as bizarre as the Express". So let me offer one final suggestion that might make the most sense of all: Let's quit seeing our pain as our foe, a serpent to stamp underfoot. Pain is not the end of the world – it's the beginning of a new and better one.

Think of the agony of childbirth – no one would willingly invite that – but on the other side is new life. And, that's true of all the pains in our life; a small birthing wants to happen.

Pain is the road to enlightenment – look it square in the face and GO FOR IT! Rather than numb or anesthetize yourself, listen to the message it's giving. "There's a emotion I'm not willing to feel."

Go within and remember any recent hurts: An insult, a slight, some guilt. Because it didn't rise to the conscious mind, (we stopped it before we could react with a scream, "That hurts! You're mean! I'm sorry!") it is energy locked in our body. Like anything caught, it is struggling. Wouldn't you if you were trapped?

That's the *pain* you're feeling. Emotion is energy in motion and wants to escape its biological way through sound, movement and tears, so let it. Go into the pain and react like a baby, be as infantile as you can be. And I can almost promise you, the pain will go away.

Some or most may find this absurd, but some will see a kernel of truth. Technology has taken us to space stations and back, but it cannot erase our pain. Let's quit looking for the answer out there, as if the government, the doctor, the minister, the priest, has more power than we do. Keep the child spontaneously alive and let's mature into finished adults. We have the answers for ourselves within, and no outside authority should reign. That's what I think was meant when He said, "Have no other gods before Me."

God lives in our hearts and speaks through our hearts as surely as He did to Jesus. Let's listen, like Jesus, to all of the messages, the good, the bad and the ugly and express them safely out. Let's quit thinking God only loves us when we're nice, polite and sweet. He loves us even more when we're rageful and sobbing and shaking, because at last we're being truthful with Him, admitting what He already knows.

Jesus established a blueprint of all that we can be. Because He respected all the emotions in his soul, had He *turned on* His full DNA? If man has the electric potential to achieve one quadrillion volts, is that why they said He *glowed*? Do we have the courage to purge out our darkness and flesh out His blueprint of light? This 21st Century could finally see His awesome prophecy fulfilled. We, like He, will do what He did and miracles will begin to unfold.

Chapter 20

Slogging Safely through Your Internal Swamp

I assume there are a variety of reactions that my readers are having to this book:

- The girl's been screaming in the woods too long and now her brains are fried – goodbye.

- I like her idea about releasing our rage but those Universal Laws just lost me.

- I've known this with every cell of my body since the moment I was born, and *finally* someone is agreeing.

Well, if you're still here and anything like me, you are eager to start your engines. I always dreaded Shakespeare in school (Kevin will hate me for this) because it took *forever* to finally get to the point. "The quality of mercy is not strained." Great! I can use that! Did it have to take two hours? And maybe that's how you feel about the meanderings of this book, so without further ado, let's begin:

If you want me to summarize, like my astrologer did for me, just remember the new three *Rs:*

Recognize
Respect
Release your feelings (privately)

Or... when in doubt, *BLOW IT OUT!*

And now, I'll elaborate:

1. Daily ask your Higher Power (God, Big Holy, Great Spirit, etc.) to increase the awareness of your feelings. Trust me, you will need the help – it's too hard to do it alone. Ask yourself dozens of times each day, "What *is* it that I am feeling"? Our ability to feel has atrophied but will sharpen with attention and desire. The good feelings you'll savor, the bad ones you'll notice, and be willing, simply, to name them.

2. Say to yourself, "I'm angry/sad/frightened/ jealous/resentful/bitter/etc. right now. And it's O.K. to be feeling that emotion – I love every feeling I have."

3. Never, never, never throw this emotion at anyone. Physics tells us there are no straight lines – *everything* returns to us. I don't want to be accosted in a shop one day because somebody's husband misinterpreted these words as encouragement to deck his boss. Go to a place where you won't disturb – your car, your bedroom, your bathroom, or outside.

4. Throw your head out the window (climb out of your intellect); it will try to interfere. Keep enough to be sensible and safe.

5. Begin breathing deeply to allow your feelings to surface, if you find this increases your sensitivity. If not, ignore and go on to 6.

6. Take the picture out of when you were small and *do* what this child wants to *do*. If you can be heard, yell into your hand and only hit things that are soft. Don't listen to yourself, don't censor yourself; the wilder and crazier, the better, as long as it's sincere. Remember to *go for the tears* – they are the major transformers. Most anger and aggression are cover-ups to avoid admitting our pain. Stay with it as long as it takes. It may take one minute, or five, or fifty and there may be more tomorrow. Or, maybe very little will happen and that's a healing too; sometimes just a tear or two is all that needs to be noticed. And sometimes, nothing perceptible will occur, but the act of naming and allowing will bring the unconscious up to the conscious. (This stuff's been in there for a very long time – even in the womb we had traumas – so patience is the name of the game.)

7. Drink plenty of water, so you don't get dehydrated, and you should be feeling fine.

Keep in mind – emotion is a powerful force. If you know you have a heart condition, do this with respectful caution. Go slowly with tiny doses at first. Take your time, no need for hurry – even small amounts are effective. I've been clearing for twenty years now and I still have more to go. You know your health and your own ability to engage in this process of cleanse, so pace yourself accordingly and continue with the assistance of your physician.

Now, calmly, or better tonight after dinner when perspective has been restored, look at the emotion, the energy to act, your signal from God to change, and ask, "What should I be changing?" Here's where your now-returned head will help. "I need to stop Fred from insulting me. What is the best way to do this?" There are many programs for conflict management that are good for children and youth. But, they don't work for adults in the long run, if it's indicative of a deeper problem.

Remember what was previously said in chapter 13, how most of us have unconscious fears that appear as a recurring pattern? Well, here is a place where the logical mind can happily do its thing. Use it to discover if there's a pattern that's occurring (meaning, you're attracting this adversity as an opportunity to flush out feelings. Remember – *negative events happen as opportunities to release emotion.)* But, if you've been honest with your examination and feel it is not a pattern, but an isolated event, then first of all, purge out the feelings in the privacy of your own safe space.

Then go to that person when you are calm and talk to him like a brother. Tell him sincerely how his behavior makes you feel, not attacking or making him wrong, just talking about your feelings and your own experience. Then tell him that the harm he's causing will definitely return to him

– that no action is lost or unseen or unac-
counted for. Then, (if he hasn't decked you
by now), you could possibly loan him this book
(or use it to block his fist). He's only harming
you as a way of releasing *his* pain inside.
(Then, it's OK to beat a hasty retreat before
any more SMuT hits the fan!)

Then, pray for him, give it over to God and
be ready to see an improvement. You aren't responsible for his reaction to this, you're only responsible to tell him the truth of how you feel
and see things, and that, only after having done
the homework, looking for a pattern in any event
that tells us its really *our* problem.

Now, if that happily engaged logical mind
tells us it *is* our problem, we can solve it with
Universal Law (Oh, no – those weird laws again.)
I'll try to be clearer this time.

Since what you put out comes back to you,
then Fred is insulting you because you've been
unconsciously feeling "I deserve to be insulted",
or some other self-deprecation. Remember: *It
only hurts if you think it's true.* Deep down you
feel worthy of insult, because as a child you accepted that identity and the pain that accompa-
nied such a thought. Since like attracts like, your
thinking attracts Fred, who also feels like you do
(worthy of insults). Why else would he be bug-
ging you? He sees himself in you.

If someone is attacking you, he already feels
like the loser. Something you're doing is threatening him – why else would he be so defensive? Now

since "What you resist, persists", you can rail against Fred till the cows come home, but it won't fix what needs to be fixed – your self-perception. If you send out a barrage of resistance, it may get the boss to fire Fred. But Fred, like JoBo, is a catalyst from you, a messenger from your unconscious, to finally acknowledge your pain.

Fred may indeed exit the scene, but the purpose of his mission will be lost. Since first we are Spirit that continually strives for wholeness (holiness), then the next person to nest into Fred's cubicle will be someone eerily like him. This pattern will continue until you change yourself.

Remember, Life is a Mirror. ***The amount of negativity within us is the amount we will see before us.*** From within to without, always. The only way to end the pain out there is to end the pain inside.

Other people's negative behavior (directed toward you) *is a reflection of your own inner thinking.* If someone is very demanding of you, it's because (unconsciously) you're very demanding of yourself. You're carrying a *charge* of anger/sorrow over the pain of excess self-demands, so you've drawn a partner (an angel in disguise) that will force these charges out. But what do we do? We miss the opportunity by putting the blame *out there.* "My life would be so much better if the people around me would change." How often have we heard ourselves say that?

Here's what *will* change events. Write down all the things that your partner/boss/friends do that drive you up the wall. State it clearly. "She demands too much of me." "He expects me to be perfect." "They think I'm stupid." Now go through the list replacing the pronouns he, she and they with *I*, because that's really what's happening. Your subconscious mind wants to release this charge so it draws the people to you who will *force* it on out. Realize they are voicing your unconscious thoughts. Tat Twam Asi - That Thou Art.

Find some time and a private place and release the feelings they've caused. You've carried this doubt and fear for years and now you can let it go and thank these people for helping.

Now that is the permanent, successful way to not only end the injury, but bring brightness to the quality of your life. As negativity leaves, it's replaced by the positive, hence only positive can be drawn to your life. Do you see? It's actually quite simple – not easy, but simple.

It's not easy because we've been indoctrinated to be strong, invincible, impervious. But if we can see a connection between rigidity and our troubles and illness, isn't it time to break free? America, in its infancy, required strength and fortitude to prosper. For two hundred years we've prized dominance and aggression as our noblest attributes. Isn't it time, as we enter the next century, to redress this costly imbalance?

I personally feel the most important quality a human can possess is love, and their ability to daily express it. Our greatest value is not what we *know*, but how much we are capable of *feeling*.

144

I know it's hard to build a mansion.
It's hard to buy an XKE.
It's hard to be a movie star,
  and it's hard to get a Ph.D.

But show me someone who does not pass judgment. Show me someone who can cry. Show me someone who can forgive twice and thrice, someone who admits his mistakes. Someone who takes responsibility for his life and doesn't play the victim or blame. Someone who is open, vulnerable, defenseless. Someone who is humble – that's hard.

"Humility – that low, sweet root –
from which all heavenly virtues shoot." [1]

Humus, the earth, being humble, is the precursor to unconditional love. Love is far more than a feeling – it's a big time, heavy-duty verb. And the only way we can do it full-time is to firstly love ourselves. It's the only reason we've failed – we don't love ourselves because we mistakenly believe that only half of us should be loved – the 'nice' part.

If we can begin to allow and include
  that half of ourselves we deny,
  that half in the dark in caverns and caves
  who was secreted rudely away.

---

[1] Marianne Moore

If we could shine light
   on our own inner child,
   hiding punished, trembling in the dark.
And call up the courage to free him,
   embrace him,
   and welcome what he needs to express.
To cherish his sorrow, anguish and fears
   as much as we treasure his smile.
To apologize for our unwitting cruelty
   in banishing him for his pain.

To promise that never again he'll be lonely,
   shunned and separated from our love.
That no matter how rageful
   and trembling he is,
   we will, humbly, fold him in our arms.

And holding him safely
   so he can drop all his fear,
   he'll cry us the river within.

Now that is love, and that is hard. But
that is our only healing.

Chapter 21

Who Can See the Invisible
Can Do the Impossible
...or Intention Changes Physics

With a final effort to speak, I plead, bring passion into your life. If you're going to be happy, be ecstatic! If you're going to be angry, be rageful! (Privately, please.) Why not work, play, sing, dance, laugh, weep, passionately? There's a Zorba awaiting in each of us. Why do you suppose the Italians have such low incidence of disease? Appassionato is their middle name!

People either experience life or stand back and safely observe. Jump in! You won't drown. I'm more concerned for you if you don't.

Sex is an inflated issue for many because when else do we surrender to abandon? As children, when we got too silly, or goofy or joyful or excited, what happened? We were told to "Hold it down!" or were punished with shame, or made to feel embarrassed for excess glee. And all of it was experienced as this message: "Don't feel too much; you'll get hurt."

So we tiptoe through our sensual world (and sensual is far more than sex – it's the paradise of our six senses), mortified we might feel too much and once again feel pain.

Well we might! We might get deeply close and vulnerable, then end up with a broken heart.

But the good news this book offers you is the tools to get through anything. Humans don't die of a broken heart because we feel too much; our hearts burst from *carrying* our sorrow because we don't feel out enough.

Sin in Latin means "short of God" and our shortness is our constant lying, to ourselves, to others and to God, about what we truly feel. We fall woefully back when we turn a deaf ear toward half of the messages He sends us. If truth is the song of the Bible we read, let's ask Him for the courage to be honest...

Each one of us willing to unchain our demons, to let free our portion of the collective sorrow, is bringing more peace to the world because everything is connected. Not only will this elevate the quality of our lives, it will decrease the cause of war. Can we do it for our brothers if not ourselves?

I challenge America, the spiritual leader, to dedicate the year 2000 – the portal of a new millennium – to a purge, a cleansing, a truth-telling, an admitting, an integration of our *silenced soul*. It is the Chinese Year of the Dragon; and having been taught by most religions and sects that our challenge was to slay this beast, what a polarized shift to recognize that his disappearance awaits our embracement.

I'm a deeply passionate person. It's been said of me, "you take folks to the edge – you're fine, we fall off". So that's why I've written this book – to share with you the tools I've used that can help you through drama and trauma.

And you'll find, when you arrive at the farthest edge of your fearsome, feeling frontier, you'll be shocked to discover you won't fall off. Like the pupae who is willing to spend time in the dark, or the Phoenix, consumed by flames, you'll awaken one morning with wings.

Does that sound preposterous, the ability to fly? As a result of twenty years of honoring my emotions, I've often experienced weightlessness, upon waking and in meditation.

Let's title the next century "Remembering the Magic", for deep within our collective unconscious we remember that magic is real – that first we are Spirit, which comes from God which is energy, light and love. Quantum Physics has lately discovered what the sages of long ago knew. Even matter, which we thought was solid, is nothing but energy, energy.

The wizard within us can mold it. We are Shape-Shifters of the highest order. Since thinking and feeling are creating our reality, why rest 'till we create the best?

Because Earth is the realm of free will, what happened in our past was the direct result of what we collectively *unconsciously* agreed upon. In order to create a more radiant future, we need only *consciously* agree – design and implement as sophisticated a peace plan as those of our military strategists. By millions of people praying and visualizing with a clear and determined intent, there is no problem that cannot be solved. Bad isn't caused by the majority of people – it's the majority of people doing nothing, and inertia takes its toll. If we're not part of a solution we *are* part of the problem – don't kid yourself there's neutrality.

"Do not correct the bad...
instead make the good increase."

The old world, without Spirit, is dying, and from it's ashes will be born the new. The earth hasn't witnessed an adventure as spectacular as the midwifery we are performing. Instead of fearing and lamenting the death, give your hearts and hands to the new. Put on the water and roll up your sleeves because in this New World, permeated by God, nothing is impossible.

The Invitation

Oriah Mountain Dreamer
Indian Elder
May 1994

It doesn't interest me what you do for a living.
I want to know what you ache for,
  and if you dare to dream
  of meeting your heart's longing.

It doesn't interest me how old you are.
I want to know if you will risk looking
  like a fool for love, for your dreams,
  for the adventure of being alive.

It doesn't interest me
  what planets are squaring your moon.
I want to know if you have touched
  the center of your sorrow,
  if you have been opened by life's betrayals,
  or have become shriveled
  and closed for fear of further pain.

I want to know if you can sit with pain,
  mine or your own,
  without moving to hide it or fade it or fix it.
I want to know if you can be with JOY,
  mine or your own,
  if you can dance with wildness
  and let the ecstasy fill you
  to the tips of your fingers and toes
  without cautioning us to be careful, be realistic,
  or to remember the limitations
  of being human.

It doesn't interest me
  if the story you're telling me is true.

I want to know if you disappoint another
  to be true to yourself,
  if you can bear the accusation
  and not betray your own soul.

I want to know if you can be faithful,
  and therefore be trustworthy.
I want to know if you can see beauty
  even when it is not pretty every day,
  and if you can source your life
  from ITS presence.
I want to know if you can live with failure,
  yours or mine,
  and still stand on the edge of the lake,
  and shout to the silver of the full moon, "YES."

It doesn't interest me to know where you live
  or how much money you have.
I want to know if you can get up
  after a night of grief and despair,
  weary and bruised to the bone,
  and do what needs to be done for the children.
It doesn't interest me who you are
  or how you came to be here.
I want to know if you will stand
  in the center of the fire with me
  and not shrink back.

It doesn't interest me where or what or with whom
  you have studied.
I want to know what sustains you from inside
  when all else falls away.
I want to know if you can be alone with yourself,
  and if you truly like the company you keep
  in the empty moments.

Suggested Reading

Talking with Angels ...... Gita Mallasz

Learning to Love Yourself ...... Gay Hendricks

Awakening to Zero Point ......Gregg Braden

The P'taah Tapes ...... Jani King

Lazy Man's Guide to Enlightenment ......Thaddeus Golas

Walking Between the Worlds ......Gregg Braden

You Can Heal Your Life ...... Louise Hay

The Findhorn Garden ...... Findhorn Community

Behaving as if the God in All Life Mattered..... Michelle Wright

The Elves of Lily Hill Farm...... Penny Kelly

Vision ...... Ken Carey

The Starseed Transmissions ...... Ken Carey

Handbook for the Ascension ...... Tony Stubbs

Kinship with All Life ...... J. Allen Boone

Song of the Soul...... Angelina

The Holotropic Mind...... Stan Grof

"Holotropic Breathwork" (Video)...... Mead Training Systems, New Canaan, CT 06840

About the Author

Cynthia Herman lives under towering oaks with her four-legged, feathered and furred friends and the spirit of Angeline. All are home and all are happy.

Her second bliss is *talking* about her book. If you wish to schedule a seminar or speaking engagement, write Earth Mirth or visit the Website.

Because of its inspired rhythmic quality, the author recommends *hearing* the book . "The voice is the audible vibration of the soul." Audio cassettes are available from Earth Mirth, either by mail or on the Web..

Earth Mirth Adventure
P.O. Box 4231
Peoria, IL 61607 6 1605
www.EarthMirth.com

1002
Pierce

309 6974288

From
Earth Mirth Adventure

Sound, Movement and Tears
by Cynthia Herman

Available in Book or on Cassette Tapes

Ordering Information

Please send the following:

_____Copies of The Book: *SM&T*
$ 14.95 each   _____

_____ Cassette Tapes: *SM&T*
$ 19.95 each   _____

Subtotal:_____

Shipping & Handling:
Bookrate: $2
Priority Mail: 1-2 books $4, 3 or more $6   **S&H:**_____

Illinois Sales Tax, please add 7%:   _____

US Check or Money Order Enclosed:_____

Name: _____

Address: _____

City, State, Zip: _____

Mail to: Earth Mirth Adventure
P.O. Box 4231
Peoria, IL 61607   *Thank You!*